Forgiven

A journey through love, pain and self-discovery

NAJAH A. WILLIAMS

 FriesenPress

Suite 300 - 990 Fort St
Victoria, BC, V8V 3K2
Canada

www.friesenpress.com

ISBN
978-1-5255-3431-7 (Hardcover)
978-1-5255-3432-4 (Paperback)
978-1-5255-3433-1 (eBook)

1. BIOGRAPHY & AUTOBIOGRAPHY, WOMEN

Distributed to the trade by The Ingram Book Company

Table of Contents

Prologue vii

Chapter 1 1
THE STORM

Chapter 2 9
THE AFTERMATH

Chapter 3 31
THE BLISS

Chapter 4 45
THE CHANGE

Chapter 5 57
THE REALITY

Chapter 6 69
THE TRUTH

Chapter 7 83
THE INSANITY

Chapter 8 91
THE FEAR

Chapter 9 125
THE CHOICE

Chapter 10. 135
THE FORGIVENESS

Chapter 11. 145
THE PURPOSE

About the Author 155

Dedicated to my beautiful daughters and charming son who believed in me when I no longer had the vision to see my project manifest. You add extraordinary value to my life and developing your character is a major part of my divine purpose. It is with great honor to love, teach and guide you.

In loving memory of my angels who have flown
and whose memories forever live on.

-Rest in Paradise-

Prologue

OFTEN WE FORGET the simple things. Things that once meant the most to us. As I sit with my ankles crossed on a floral-patterned fleece blanket I've spread upon the fresh cut grass, I can't help but look around. I see the young men playing basketball shirtless on the court, a couple pushing their restless toddler daughter on the vibrant colored swing set, and a father catching his anxious daughter at the bottom of the slide. I crack a smile as I listen to the sound of the many birds whistling in sync throughout the trees, while shamelessly indulging in the scent of fresh pine from the surrounding forests.

While the simplicity of nature is mesmerizing, the best part is when I recline back onto the soft blanket with my big brown eyes to the infinite sky. Looking up, I see a shade of blue so tranquil and beautiful that only our creator could make. The temperature outside is seventy-two degrees, slightly breezy and mostly sunny. My big, kinky, curly hair is blowing with the touch of each key stroke. In my mind I'm envisioning and reminiscing of the deep stroke that put me to a sound sleep last night.

So, who am I? I'm just like you. While you may not be a 5'9" African-American woman in her early thirties, you and I are both temporal and we both have at some point experienced a degree of love and an analogous degree of desolation and pain. When we're emotionally hurt, we find we are more subjective to vulnerability, or at least that's what we convince ourselves. So many times, we are fraid of our own truths that we look for answers everywhere but within us. It took for me to go through nearly two decades of hurt and pain before I learned most of my pain and misery was created by me. In those leading moments, I discovered that I held the secret to my own happiness the entire time. The beauty about life is that we are all unique and we have our own divine purpose to fulfill. And in getting there, everyone has their own personal story created by them and told through them.

As the beauty of life amazes me, I can't help but think of the reality that lies back at home. The reality that I'm in my thirties, I'm at my wit's end in my marriage, transitioning between careers, and still trying to "figure out" life's next move. One thing for certain is that life is about choices, and your choices determine your destiny. I own my decisions, both good and bad. I want to live; I want to do the things that make me most happy. I'm emotionally-driven with an insatiable curiosity, and while at times I can be a bit overly defensive and sensitive, its only because of my desire for genuine, incontestable love.

No person *wants* to work at a job they despise and dread just for a mere check. If you, like most of us, *must* invest forty to sixty hours a week in doing something, there should at least be some degree of gratification beyond financial. Living a fulfilling life is about making the choices that align with your destination. I don't want easy as *most* things worth having will take hard work to not only get, but to maintain. So often I'm mistaken for being condescending. But the reality is, I'm quite the opposite. Do I have expectations for and from my life? Yes. And I've learned to not apologize for fulfilling my dreams.

While I've come to know the true value of my inner beauty and my worth (*which cannot be justified materialistically*), I can't help but ponder on the fact that the truth remains the same. So how did I go from making a competitive annual salary, vacationing in Miami and cruising regularly, to being alone and losing a grip on the things that meant the most to me? Life hit me like a speeding train all at once, but I will take it back to November 2015 …

"I don't see why we have to go to school when Thanksgiving break is only a few days away," mumbled Jada, my nine-year-old mini-me.

"You're going to school and this is non-negotiable. You girls played in the pool all night knowing we'd be flying back to Memphis at five in the morning, *knowing* school starts at eight a.m. So, yes! I will be outside in the truck waiting on you two," I said to my little queens as I prepared to take them to their preparatory academy.

I sat in the driver's seat and pulled down my mirrored sun visor to apply my favorite cocoa shade of lipstick that complemented my medium-brown skin tone. As I watched my girls walk back inside through the rearview mirror, the thought of not being in their lives brought an instant chill to my spine and pain to my heart.

The more I replayed last night over in my mind, the more disgusted I became with myself. After spending four fabulous days in Daytona Beach and Universal Studios with my family, an unexplainably intense feeling hit my heart … like a part of me died instantly.

I found myself knee deep in the Atlantic Ocean at midnight contemplating suicide and I didn't even know why. A non-holy spirit came upon me that I couldn't explain … like something was telling me that I couldn't go on anymore. My husband followed me out the beachfront hotel and stood in the sand as I explored the unfamiliar waters.

He fearlessly tested my insanity, allowing me to venture out into the ocean waters. When he saw I showed no fear of depth nor death, he quickly rushed in, pulling me ashore before I went to the point of no return. I can't swim. He insisted it was just a phase—a pre-midlife crisis of some sort—but I couldn't ignore it, couldn't shake it, or put my finger on it. Then came the storm of life.

Chapter 1

THE STORM

L IKE CLOCKWORK, MY bladder wakes me up every morning faithfully in the early two o'clock hour to use the bathroom. This particular morning when I awoke, there was a continual blue light gleaming from my husband's side of the room.

"TJ wake up … baby get up," I said as I nudged my husband in his side while he slept serenely. He lay there motionless. He'd only been home for a couple of hours.

I knew he was exhausted. His nine-year-old daughter, my only step-daughter, got hurt earlier at school that day. He sat at the children's hospital with her for several hours. I offered to accompany him, but he insisted I stay home. He didn't know how long the parent's presence would be required, and he didn't want me to be away from the kids for too long. Although my husband and I have no 'biological' children together, he has been an energizing part of our lives for the last seven years. I love his two children as I do my own.

I tried to wake him to let him know that his phone was doing something, but he didn't budge. *He must have left his phone in his jeans when he got into the bed.* I started to make my way to the bathroom on the opposite side of the room. I stopped dead in my tracks when I indeed confirmed that I heard his phone vibrating. Immediately I thought it was something urgent at that time of morning, especially considering the incident with his daughter. I bent down to pick up his pants and his cell phone fell to the cold hardwood floor. When I picked his phone up, I could feel the vibrations in my palm. My heart dropped when I turned it over.

Words cannot describe my disappointment and hurt to see that it was an incoming call from his ex-mistress in the wee hours of the morning. My first thought was to answer the phone as I thought the affair ended years ago, but the shock wouldn't allow me to come to terms with the fact that she was *still* in his life and her contact name was saved as "wifey." My issue was not with her at that point. I can't control the agenda of a wicked or promiscuous woman. My issue was with the man who I made a commitment to and desired loyalty from above all. He had an affair with her less than a year after we got married and she managed to pop-up sporadically over the years. He always dismissed it as a coincidence and insisted she meant nothing, but deep down inside I always had that gut feeling that she would eventually pop-up again … and again.

Once the phone stopped vibrating, I took a deep breath and proceeded to unlock his phone with our mutual unlock code—our anniversary. I went to his text messages and saw a series of new text messages.

Wifey: "The baby is coming!!!" 1:51a.m.

Wifey: Image (Photo of her in a hospital room in a gown holding her stomach) 2:25a.m.

Wifey: "Where r u babe? U said u were coming rite back." 2:38a.m.

I dropped his phone onto the hardwood floor in our bedroom. What was once clear was now a haze as I looked around the room in despair. I looked over at him sleeping peacefully in our bed, not bothered by the noise or turmoil brewing inside me. I thought about all the things that I could do to him while he lay asleep without a care in the world. All of the things I should do to him in this moment. A cast iron skillet to the head, hot grits to his chest, or Lorena Bobbitt to the dick to name a few. I thought about how I'd invested the last six years into a marriage that appeared perfect to the world, yet was a lie being lived every day.

I picked up his phone off the floor and I invaded his privacy as if it was my given right to do so. I walked over to him slowly. I took a deep breath as my chest pounded heavily. I forcefully threw his phone at his bare chest. He awoke abruptly.

"What's wrong baby?" he asked astonished as he started to sit upright and squint his eyes.

He could see the hurt and pain in my face. I was beyond tears as I had been through so much that I couldn't shed another. I leaned over to him and whispered into his ear.

"Get your shit and get the fuck out of this house. Don't make a scene and don't get loud with me."

The kids were asleep and I wanted them to stay that way. His phone continued to vibrate and after he unlocked his phone, reality became transparent as he sat in silence. He saw where I screenshot their text thread over the last two weeks and sent the images to my phone. I didn't care enough to delete the messages from his sent folder either. I wanted him to know I saw everything and I knew everything. Also, just in case I needed evidence to prove infidelity in court, I had all the proof I needed.

He sat at the foot of the bed and watched as I paced back and forth. Neither one of us was certain as to what I was going to do. Of all the things he could say, when he finally spoke he said, "So you're really going to throw our marriage away all because of a pregnant hoe lying on me?"

I looked at him and laughed at the way he insulted my intelligence. I laughed at the way he thought I would sweep this under the rug like every other act of infidelity. I read how he said that he was happy she was having his child and they're a family. I synced my iPhone to my Bluetooth speaker and began listening to Sade. I packed his belongings, although many of his personal items were still in the oversize suitcase from the trip we'd literally just gotten back from. Tears streamed down his face as he pleaded to talk to me about the situation at hand. I walked past him as if he didn't exist to me anymore. I heard the kids awakening in their rooms but urged them to go back to bed. It was only 4 a.m. at that time and too early for them to be up.

I locked myself in the bathroom and cried the tears that I didn't know I had remaining in me. I had to be at work at 6 a.m. but couldn't bear to face him—the world—anyone. I stared into the mirror and saw a face I could no longer recognize. My pain was written all over my face. I felt so much shame, hurt, and embarrassment. *How could this have gone on for this long? How could he lie about his daughter being injured? How could he have been so reckless and so damn careless? How could he bring another life into this world when he has a whole family at home? I worked hard as the breadwinner and rarely asked him to contribute financially. I went into debt to build his damn cleaning business from the ground up, and for what? How could I hide this from the world like I'd done in the past?*

The questions were endless, though I never questioned God despite the hurt being painfully overwhelming. I called my immediate supervisor and was instructed to take some time off from work, as much time as needed to figure things out and recuperate.

One day off turned into three weeks off and before I knew it, Christmas was only a couple weeks away. I hid from my family and friends. I shut everyone out of my life seeking solitude and peace within. Despite all the things that I erased, the truth was something that couldn't be.

It's ironic because a year or so prior to the ultimate lovechild affair, an incident involving a dating app and multiple women occurred, and he reassured me that it was never anything physical or sexual. He said that it was just for *entertainment*. I worked a lot and was oftentimes tired. Nothing but messages and pictures were exchanged, so no harm done he insisted. I know that as humans no one is perfect, so I chose to accept the situation and work on getting us back on track. I found a reputable therapist and it took months of begging and pleading before he agreed to go. But he finally agreed.

TJ was very indifferent about going to counseling as he felt it would be another episode of the blame game, shaming and antagonizing him. I do recall one specific counseling session that we attended. During the entire session, TJ was quiet for the most part and when he did speak, he spoke as if he was genuinely apologetic for the affairs and pain caused as a result. At one point however, he told the therapist that "If you go looking for something, you will find it."

The doctor asked me how I felt about that statement. My reply was, "I think its bullshit. If I go outside looking for a million dollars, will I stumble across it? No. If something isn't there, then it simply isn't there. Point being, if you're doing nothing then there is nothing to hide. If I'm loyal in my marriage, there is no way he could pick up my phone and magically signs of infidelity appear all because he went on a quest to find something."

As time began to pass, I knew I had enough vacation time and sick time accumulated to cover my absence, but on the same token, all the free time on my hands was driving me insane. It drove me crazy because I wondered if he was with her. I wondered if going back was even a considerable option at that point. I passed time by making hand poured massage oil candles and sitting at the park for hours at a time, writing and reading. I passed time by not acknowledging my emotional state and just hoping it would go back to *normal* on its own.

Less than a week after finally returning to work, I had an unexpected visit from a woman I was unfamiliar with. I overheard her specifically requesting my presence as the matter at hand was urgent. She asked me if I could step away since it was a private matter.

I agreed and we stepped outside the building. She introduced herself, using only her first name—Angela—as if I was to automatically know who she was. She then proceeded to remind me of the text messages she and I exchanged a couple months ago regarding TJ. But there had been so many women, I honestly had no recollection of any of it.

Angela stated she had to do this in person and waited as long as she could, but I needed to know that *my* husband was the father of her daughter. The baby was only three months old at the time, making both of his new additions only three months apart in age.

In its purest form of honesty, I was still so incredibly numb from everything transpiring in my life that it didn't immediately register, so I showed no emotion or regard to the matter that she was trying to discuss.

I was very nonchalant and informed her that her *alleged* child with TJ was not my problem as we were no longer together due to the bombshell of another baby and I walked away. She attempted to show me text messages and pictures of him with *their* child to confirm, but they were all so irrelevant at that point.

Needless to say when confronted with the truth, there was total denial across the board from TJ. It was then I realized that you can't want or expect more for people than they want or expect for themselves. We are who we are individually and just because we have certain values, morals, and beliefs, we can't expect others to share them, accept them or agree with them. Clear communication is critical in any successful relationship. Whether it be home, work, school, etc. Clear communication removes misconceptions as it's open, honest, and unfiltered. It doesn't mean that you must be obscene or offensive, simply be a person of good character. Say what you mean and mean what you say. Stand by your word as it goes hand-in-hand with action when it comes to defining your character.

As the new year approached, I was too afraid of what the future held, so I chose to live in the fears of the past. My fear gave me permission to withdraw from life and I felt the misery of my isolation and loneliness. So, I went back to the only thing that made sense, the only thing that seemed safe to me in a world filled with chaos and deceit. I went to TJ for comfort and familiarity, sneaking and creeping with my own husband as I knew he'd taken on the role as a new father and forced provider.

While I don't fault myself for seeking his presence as I value marriage and what it stands for, I do fault myself for not allowing myself adequate time to heal emotionally. I wanted to be with him for all the wrong reasons. I wanted to be with him because I didn't want him to be with *them*. I wanted to be with him because I didn't know how to be without him … because I didn't want to feel defeated.

I knew that the pain was real because I felt it every time I looked at him, every time I thought about the babies. But there was always this unrealistic, deranged part of me that thought this wound would heal on its own as the human body possesses an astonishing capacity to heal itself. I waited and waited for something that never occurred. The days turned into weeks which turned into months. We were just holding onto hope, too afraid to let go. While I knew that he was whole-heartedly putting forth a genuine effort to mend our shattered relationship, it just wasn't enough, or maybe it was just too late. I knew what I needed, but I masked my feelings behind what I felt I wanted at the time.

Don't misunderstand me when I say that I was totally blinded by the infidelities. My husband is 6'2", dark chocolate skinned tone, slim to medium build and has the potential to be a good mate. He has secrets, insecurities, and a past like we all do, so perfection was never my objective as I too am perfectly imperfect. However, when I say he's a good man, I mean the brotha hustles hard in the streets, cooks gourmet meals, cleans the house from top to bottom like we have a maid service, loves to organize, runs my bath water, helps with the kids' homework and projects, pampers me like we are still in the honeymoon phase, puts it down like he deserves the crown, and is protective like a soldier. He is all of that and beyond. The man even combs my daughters' hair in styles that are often complimented, and I'm not talking that blow-and-go hair. I'm talking grease, edge control, barrettes, and old-fashioned straightening combs. I honestly don't know how or even when he managed to find the time to be both *my* husband and *their* lover, but somehow this life sort of just happened, and this is just the aftermath.

Chapter 2

THE AFTERMATH

ABOUT SEVEN MONTHS after our initial separation, we both felt that it wasn't fair to walk away from our marriage without giving it a fight, especially considering how I dreaded the thought of starting over and had nothing more to lose.

I dreaded the thought of getting to know someone, trusting someone, having to meet their family and be looked down upon for my flaws. Having to apologize for things that I'm not really sorry for. It all seemed like too much of a hassle and just not worth the emotional investment. So, I chose to settle for being emotionless. I chose to be okay with *not* being okay.

The hurt overruled the love and the atmosphere was intolerable at times. He did everything that he knew to try and regain my trust, but for every big victory, there was always a small disappointment that got the best of me. There were always questions and uncertainties and it hurt me to know that I couldn't just flip an "off/on" switch and be *normal* again. I wanted so hard to forgive, move on, and give my marriage a fair shot. I wanted to be the virtuous woman of meekness that I saw reflected in my mother, but I allowed my circumstances to dictate my every decision.

I was there physically, but mentally I left the marriage when that cold reality set in. I played the victim instead of the victor and it was the start of a long and painful death of a marriage. I condemned him for the same thing that he apologized for every day and that wasn't fair to him.

After about another year of mutually holding onto unhealthy pains and aggressions, we decided that for what it was potentially worth, a vacation for old time sake would be refreshing and may be what we needed to rekindle the dying romance. When we were good, we were great, but when it rained, it stormed, it flooded, it caused tsunamis. I wanted a strong marriage with moments of pain, not a painful marriage with a few good moments.

We vacationed in Mexico. The same spot we'd visited several times in the past. Nevertheless, even on a private island, we were still like walking time bombs just waiting to explode. Every little thing that we did ticked the other one off as we fought to tolerate each other.

I can remember searching for a signal to connect with my family and friends via social media once we got situated in our suite in Mexico, and I can remember his rage as a result. He wasn't into social media and respectively asked that I either limit my interactions or simply not include him in what I chose to "share". That was always the rule and I always chose to abide.

This particular time, I posted a picture of myself on the patio smiling with a glass of Moscato in hand as my *Bon Voyage*. He instantly became upset and my rage was at the point of no return.

I felt as if he didn't want "people" to see, or at least believe that we were happy. I have insecurities as we all do and only wanted reassurance, at least when it came down to what mattered to my heart. The continuous disrespect from the ghetto baby mamas', along with the lack of communication and inconsistencies created a deep wedge between us. Not to mention, the two women were equally infuriated by my tenacity. You'd almost think that I was the one who'd gotten pregnant by *their* husband.

Words meant nothing, and action was never taken to give me the reassurance my heart desired.

As time progressed, I did the inevitable and proposed an open marriage as divorce was already on the table and remained unfavorable between the two of us. The very thought of sharing *me* made him sick to his stomach. He couldn't fathom the thought of another man taking pleasure in *his* wife.

At the time I believed, or at least tried to convince myself that if I gave him permission to step outside our marriage for sex, then it wouldn't be so painful when and if it occurred. I did research and found a lot of success stories with open marriages and even made a contingent list of rules for us to abide by *if* consent was mutual.

Needless to say, we never came to a mutual agreement and the concept was soon gone with the wind. I worked overtime to keep my mind off the reality of wanting to leave but being too afraid to go. I spent all of my spare time listening to old school R&B and jotting down random thoughts …

"Times Ten"

Trust broken, words unspoken
The more I drink, the clearer I think
Progress is what I thought we were making
Never did I dream that my heart would again be breaking
In the game of love and trust, lies never win
Still it hurts so much because we grew to be best friends
A wounded heart is what I once had
Yet you mended every fragile piece, proving that the good outweighed the bad
Trusting you was the most beautiful thing I learned to do
You made it so easy for me to fall back in love with you
Nothing left but the pieces of a broken heart
Tired of searching for a brand new start

How hard is it not to lie?
How many times can one person make you cry?
How many nights must you dare to ask God why?
Not realizing the damage that you've done
When all I ever wanted was to be your only one
Trying to wrap my brain around how you could tell such a lie
Wondering what it is that you're trying to hide
The way that I love you is different than before
That's why this hurts ten times much more

Unfortunately, during the midst of my initial breakdown in 2015, I picked up the notoriously criticized and deadly bad habit of smoking. Black & Mild wine cigars to be exact. I would smoke three to four full cigars a day to calm my nerves, or at least that's what I convinced myself. Nevertheless, since I'm down to only one-a-day, it's no longer a necessity, but I still sometimes enjoy stepping away from the stresses of work for a slight peace of mind via a little nicotine inhalation.

"You know smoking is bad for you," said an anticipated voice.

"And this coming from the man smoking a Newport cigarette … double standards," I responded in a sarcastic voice and used my hand to shield my flame from the wind as I lit my cigar.

He smiled at me and for the first time in a long time, I felt *seen*, although he's seen me countless times before.

"So how old are you if you don't mind me asking?" I looked into his youthful eyes.

"I'm 28. And you?"

"I'm 31."

Leonard worked nearby as a local driver and we would run into each other sporadically throughout the week. It was mainly while smoking and we would make random small talk to keep the moments from being too awkward.

I initially met Leonard a couple of months ago. It was shortly after I returned from vacationing in Mexico, and we shared our recent travel experiences. We had a lot of neat little things in common and I was amazed at how we connected so effortlessly.

There was an immediate physical attraction, but I knew that I couldn't act on it. However, this particular day, my cancer horoscope said that I would meet my "intellectual equivalent".

I know it may seem crazy or even elementary, but my horoscope is usually dead on for the most part. While it doesn't dictate me, I use it as a helpful guiding tool and it's sometimes fun to compare what really happened to what was projected.

/ I work with a lot of professional businessmen on a daily basis, so it was a very realistic prediction and it made my day suspenseful.

I spent the whole day wondering *who could this mystery person be?* No one person really connected with me on a personable level and the idea of having an intellectual conversation with another adult without arguing was inviting. The day was almost gone and I was saddened that my horoscope was wrong.

Leonard and I continued to smoke and vibe as usual. Visually judging, Leonard was the last person to come to my mind on an intellectual level as he appeared to be on the rough side, considering his multiple facial piercings and reggae presence. However, life has confirmed that you can't judge a book by its cover.

I couldn't help but foolishly think for a brief moment, *what if what I needed was right there in front of me the whole time?* Like how it sometimes turns out in the movies and in love songs. He flicked his cigarette butt and proceeded to tell me he'd see me around as he always seems to say. At this point, I knew seeing him was hit-and-miss. I was tired of anticipating his presence every day and trying to put together all these tiny pieces from every conversation to make a whole one. So, I decided to put my *big girl* panties on and step out of my comfort zone as time was always of the essence. I tossed my unfinished cigar into the sewer when I felt his goodbye approaching.

My thoughts were all over the place and for every one-second it felt like ten were passing. I took a deep breath and just went in.

"Look, I know that I don't know you very well and to tell you the truth I don't even know what I'm doing right now. I've *never* done this before, but here it goes. As you may or may not know, I am married but we're going through difficult circumstances. It's been too much for too long. I don't want or expect anything from you but there is just something about you that intrigues me, and I just want to get to know you better …"

My speech was interrupted as I was called back to work. A part of me was relieved. *This guy probably thinks I'm looney.* I have a bad habit of saying too much too soon and its usually out of innocence and nervousness. I had one foot in my marriage and the other out the door. Leonard was not a factor as the love for TJ was lost long ago … or at least believing that made me sleep better at night.

Later that day, I went outside for a final smoke break and there was a short note under the windshield wiper of my truck. The note was neatly written and it read:

"I got off early. HMU later when you get a chance. —Lenny", followed by his cell number.

I'm not sure what later meant, as I was new to this 2017 stuff as I call it. But I knew what I wanted and I didn't want to wait.

I was a go-getter at everything and he was no exception. He responded fairly quick after my first text and we continued to exchange texts back and forth over the remainder of the night. We mutually agreed to meet up with one another the next day at 7p.m. at his place.

"Come inside, " said Leonard charmingly smiling as he stood in the door of his townhome.

This man was absolutely gorgeous. Leonard is about 5'11", waist length ombre colored dreadlocks, dimples, nice physique, and the most beautiful white-chocolate mixed with caramel skin you could imagine. I usually steer away from "light-skinned" brothas as there is almost always an uncanny arrogance and cockiness about them, but I couldn't resist. His skin was smooth, hairless, flawless and covered in tattoos. His smile was bright enough to light up the stairway to heaven.

"You look very nice. Your work attire does not do you justice," he said as I walked inside past him.

I was dressed like I just came from the gym, wearing a pink and gray colored sleeveless shirt along with matching cotton leggings that looked painted on, as every woman has that one pair of pants that accentuates even the most imaginative curves.

I haven't felt desirable in a long time and it was overdue, even if it was just for a stolen moment. I could feel him looking at my ass, which was exactly what I wanted him to do. I wanted that ass to marinate on his mind. I visually inspected his domain. You could definitely tell that it was a bachelor's pad, but not in a bad way. It had a very masculine appearance and was decorated at a minimal, yet it still had a homey feel.

I slowly paced back and forth across the floor. *What am I doing?* I thought to myself. Getting there was almost too good to be true and I guess I never really gave much thought as to how I envisioned it going from that point.

"You did tell me that you're a musician," I said as I rubbed my fingers across the jagged grooves of his wooden drum sticks.

I placed the drum sticks back onto the beautiful drum set that stood front and center. He sat down in a chair that he carried from his recording area. He slid a swivel chair next to him and offered me a seat.

"I'm so sorry. I'm so nervous," I said to him as I sat down. He tilted my chin up.

"Believe it or not, for some unapparent reason, I'm nervous too. I've played in front of tens of thousands of people and I've never been nervous. Especially never when it came down to a woman … *never*," he said as he made direct eye contact with me.

My palms were becoming sweaty and I could feel the moisture between my thighs. I could see his lips moving, and hear sounds, but I just couldn't get beyond the pretty teeth and smile to make out the words, so I just nodded in agreement to whatever it was that he was saying until I was released from the trance.

"What's your zodiac sign?" I asked curiously as I spun around playfully in the chair.

"Leo. Yours?" he replied.

"Leonard the Leo, what a coincidence!" I joked.

"Me? Seriously though, I'm a sensitive, emotional, crybaby ass cancer, but I have a good heart and when I love, I love hard. I'm just often misunderstood," I said.

I asked him to direct me towards the bathroom where I did the infamous mirror and freshness check that every woman does to make sure she looks (and smells) the way that she desires too.

"Want anything to drink?" he asked through the door.

"Water please," I responded.

When I came out of the restroom he was coming from the kitchen with two glasses of ice cold water. I thanked him as he sat them down on his glass coffee table. I pulled him by the arm towards me.

"So, I guess a hug would finally be appropriate," I said shifting the vibe.

He pulled me close to him and wrapped his arms around my waist as I clinched my arms tightly around his neck. His body smelled shower fresh. I leaned in closer. *What am I doing?* I thought again as I stood here with this man that I didn't really know yet craved beyond my control. He embraced me passionately and intimately. It was a feeling of relief. He went in to kiss my lips and I allowed him too. His lips were soft and his mouth was sweet. He kissed me like I'd never been kissed before. As he pulled me in closer to him, I could feel his hand sliding down my backside, making its way around to the front.

"No, not like this," I said as I pulled away from him.

I looked around at the lack of comforting resources available and the studio equipment. He picked up on the vibe of my uneasiness. He reached for my hand and led me upstairs.

When I entered his room, I immediately noticed how organized he was. His closet was immaculate. His shoes were lined up in a straight line, and all his watches and baseball caps were neatly organized with equal spacing in between them. His walls were filled with inspirational artwork and framed quotes. There were handwritten notes and reminders randomly throughout the room. He had hundreds of amazing books on his bookshelf, although it was only Shakespeare who earned a solo spot on the top shelf. The vinyl album cover for Anita Baker's "Rapture" album was hung on the wall above an unmarked cassette tape which I later learned had a sentimental meaning. I admired the strategic placement.

"Anita is amazing. One of my absolute favorites and in my opinion, that is without a doubt her all-time best album. Your room is so eccentric. I love it!" I exclaimed.

There were several signed autographs.

"How'd you come across these?" I asked admiring a signed photo of saxophonist Kirk Whalum and admiring several framed others.

Leonard laughed and asked me to come to him. I walked across the room and we sat on his king sized sleigh bed. He pulled out his phone. He launched his Facebook app and while it hadn't been updated in over a year, it didn't stop him from having thousands of friends and followers.

"I play the drums professionally so I've met a lot of interesting people along the way, although I've never been star-struck," he said confidently as he scrolled through hundreds of pictures.

There he was … countless selfies and group pictures with A-list celebrities and fans all around the world. How amazing of an experience to headline for such titles.

"I don't want to see anymore. I get it," I said as I pushed his phone away.

I'm not sure if it was intimidation or mere jealousy. But I instantly felt like the competition for his attention would be endless with a man like him, and while I enjoyed a challenge, I just wanted to be with someone that I didn't have to sexually share with the rest of the world.

There were so many pictures of him with beautiful women from all over the world.

"How many women have you been with?" I asked him.

He chuckled slightly then kneeled between my legs and lifted my chin to force mutual eye contact.

"No. We're not about to go there because it doesn't matter. My past is my past. Do you know how easy and effortless it is for me to get women? Do you know how hard it is to meet women who aren't looking for a come up? And because I'm exposed to this celebrity lifestyle, they automatically assume that I'm some sort of a get rich quick scheme for them. They automatically assume I'm rolling in dough. Do you know how restless it gets trying to maintain a certain image for women? I'd much rather meet somebody at my regular job who doesn't already know what I do and allow them to get to know me first," he said smiling.

"Plus, let's be real … I know that you don't take me serious considering these circumstances," I said to him looking for a confirmation as I still wasn't convinced.

"I'm not going to lie to you. I've never dated or even had sex with a married woman before, not unless she didn't tell me. I mean like never ever, but for some reason, I don't mind taking this risk with you, whatever *this* turns out to be," he said. I didn't know what to say, think or do.

Lenny sat back down on the bed next to me. I reclined my body back and adjusted the pillow that he placed beneath my head. I struggled to get comfortable, turning over so that I could lay onto my stomach. He massaged and caressed my lower back as we talked. I could feel the pressure and he could feel my tension as he rubbed his hands back and forth across my fitted shirt, gradually exposing my soft, touchable skin. His touch was amazing, and I could feel the conversation becoming more easy and natural for the both of us. We continued to open up and let one another into our own worlds, picking and choosing what to admit and what to omit.

His touch turned into a soft kiss in the small of my back. I welcomed its euphoric feel. He got down onto the floor on his knees and aggressively pulled my body towards him, like a just released inmate about to eat real southern fried chicken for the first time in ten years. I lifted my chest off the bed and arched my pelvis as I felt his hands gripping my soft ass. His hands were at the top of my pants. I could feel the coolness of the air as he slowly pulled them down, kissing, caressing and massaging each cheek. He slid my panties to the side, kissing my body in every place that he allowed his hands to explore.

"You taste so good," he said as he delicately mastered the art of oral satisfaction.

My hands clinched his luxury sheets as I begged for more. He pleased and teased my body on levels that were unknown to me, but I knew how to play that game too. I pulled him to his feet by his belt. I slowly and gently ran my fingers across his skin. I raised his shirt and lightly kissed his stomach over and over, adding more suction to each kiss as I kneeled onto the floor. I stripped him of his every piece of clothing, licking my lips at the thought of how he tastes.

I looked him in the eyes as I pleasured him. I wanted him to watch me. I wanted to see the faces he made as I devoured him with precision. I wanted to feel him. I wanted to show him how much wanting *me* meant to me. With nothing but my t-shirt and panties on, I pushed him onto the bed and grinded my body on top of his. I held his face between my hands as I kissed his lips.

"I want to do this. I swear I do," he said in between kisses.

I felt a rejection coming but I continued. He finally pulled away from my kisses.

"I do, but I don't have a condom. I gave my roommate my last one the other day and I honestly didn't prepare for this to happen so soon if you know what I mean, but I want this, I want you. I can run to the store. We can go together. It's just around the corner," he said as he held my ass in his hands.

He returned his lips to mine. As much as I wanted to say "Yasss!!!" in my Wendy Williams voice, I knew that it was best to play it *safe*. Besides, I was pressed for time and I definitely didn't plan on surpassing first base so soon either. I guess I just assumed all single, good-looking, well-endowed men have an infinite supply of latex.

I instead said, "No, I completely understand. I don't know what's gotten over me. I'm so out of my element with all of *this*. Another time is cool. Besides, I said I'd be home no later than 9:30p.m. and it's already ten minutes after the hour."

I put my pants and shoes back on. We hugged and he walked me to my truck, although I insisted I was "fine" being it was pouring down rain. Thankfully I was parked under the carport, although it was no shelter against the strong wind mixed with cool, hard rain.

"Call me when you make it in!" he called out as I pulled off.

It stormed terribly on my way back home as I recklessly flew down I-240W to beat the clock like Cinderella. I had over ten missed calls and didn't want to argue any further as I contemplated what lie I would tell.

There was a lot of tension at home that night as TJ sensed I was up to something. I'm a very routine person and after living with someone for that many years, you know when they begin to do things differently. He noticed my every move and I kept the heat off me as often as I could. I picked fights over every little thing and referenced my every current action to one of his past. When I was home he was angry. When I was gone he was angry.

The very next day, TJ picked up his second youngest daughter from her mother without discussing it with me as always. The crazy part is that I practically spelled out what it would take for us to work and it was primarily transparency when it came down to his children, and financial support of some sort for *our* household. It was his birthday weekend, I had made sure that *my* kids were gone for the entire weekend, and more so, he told me that he hasn't communicated with his baby's mother in weeks.

The fighting was non-stop and it turned into a sleepless night. I overslept and was late for work the next morning and was issued a Level II warning as I, "damaged the company's brand by failing to meet the client's expectations." My rebellion and rage was at an all-time high, and to top it off, I hadn't seen or heard from Leonard since the other evening.

Unexpectedly, my bad day was beginning to turn around. Shortly after getting to work, I grabbed a cold bottle of water out the fridge and heard my phone vibrating loudly as it rested on the metal surface at the bottom of my locker. I grabbed it quickly to take a peek before someone came in as phones are prohibited for confidentiality.

Lenny: "Are you okay?"

Me: "Really?!?! I haven't heard from you since the other night."

Lenny: (Screenshots of the message thread and his call log)

Me: "Well, I didn't get any of those messages or calls but no worries. You busy?"

Lenny: "I'm working but I should be home no later than 8. You can come over if you like."

Me: "I'd love too. I will make it 8:30ish to give you time to get situated. Do you need me to bring anything?"

Lenny: "You're too sweet. No, just you."

Me: (Smiley face emoji) ☺

"You look beautiful," Leonard said as I entered his home.

He got off early and invited me to come sooner if I desired to. I conscientiously wore a mid-length denim dress with a fitted black belt around the waist. Beneath it was a black lace coordinating Victoria Secret's panty and bra set and my milk chocolate skin complimented by a splash of *Seduction* by V.S. His home was clean, quiet and dark. He asked me about my day and we made small talk for a short while. He began to open up to me about his family, his childhood, his touring experiences, and so forth. I enjoyed his conversation, although it was hard to not get lost in those eyes and that smile.

"Oooo … I almost forgot," I said as I reached into my leather handbag pulling out a gift wrapped massage oil candle. "This is for you … it's one of my *Soothing Lavender* candles, my favorite! Is it okay if I light it?" I asked.

He removed the transparent lid and sniffed the candle.

"Of course!" he said as he poured me a glass of wine.

"So, when you say *my* candle, you mean you actually made this?" he asked.

I nodded my head yes in agreeance.

"This candle smells amazing … you're amazing."

"Thanks, but I don't make them anymore."

"What, are you insane?"

"It's a long story, but in a nutshell, I no longer have my stuff and it takes money to get started all over again."

"Do you buy wholesale?"

"Yes."

"Email me the name of the company you use and the products to get you started back up. I'll order everything you need and have it shipped straight to you."

"Are you serious?"

"I'm serious baby. I got you … I promise."

Lenny inquired as to how long he had the pleasure of my presence.

"I'm all yours until about 11 o'clock," I said as I placed the candle onto his bedside table and lit it.

I glanced at my phone prior to putting it on silence and turning it facedown. I was relieved to see that it was only a quarter after nine, although it seemed like we were talking for hours already. He held my face in his hands as he kissed my lips, then smiled.

"11 o'clock is perfect, especially since I have to get up early to play. So, do you want to start watching a movie, continue to talk or just chill and listen to some music?" he asked.

"I'm a music freak so that'll always be my first choice, but I like number two *too* if that's okay with you," I told him.

He smiled as he shook his head at me. "Okay. Cool. You want me to put something on or did you want to listen to something in particular?"

"Surprise me. A person's choice of music says a lot about their personality and character," I said.

He walked over to his laptop with dual PC monitor and decided to take me back to early 90's R&B, slowing it down with Silk "Lose Control".

"Okay, you're young but you have good taste in music … so far. Besides, you're a musician after all, so I didn't expect any less," I said smiling as I grooved my head to the beat.

"Do you trust me?" he asked mischievously as he walked back over to the bed where I sat.

"Until you give me a reason not to," I responded.

"Good," he said as he got behind me and kissed my neck.

He asked me to close my eyes. The darkness came quickly as he placed a blindfold around them, securing the closure behind my head.

"Are you okay?" he asked as he reached for my hands.

I nodded that I was all right. He laid my head down onto a pillow and tied each of my wrists to each end of his open sleigh headboard.

"What are you doing?" I asked playfully.

"Don't struggle. Trust me and just relax," he said as he kissed my lips.

He unbuttoned my dress slowly. He kissed my neck down to my breasts. He used one hand to unfasten my front-closure bra while the other hand was used to pleasure me. I could feel my chest pounding as he slowly licked and sucked my hardened nipples. My moans turned him on. He untied one of my wrists. I sucked his neck and gently bit his earlobe. I begged him to let me have him at that moment as I could feel my body ready to gush in ecstatic release. Right before my moment of manual orgasm, he took an oral detour downtown, taking his time to ensure he didn't miss a beat. I pulled his long, soft dreads as I maneuvered his head, digging my nails into his shoulder with my free hand. As my body climaxed, he savored its every delight. He pleased me until I begged him to free me completely.

Once released, I tied his dreads up and laid his body down. I kissed, touched, sucked and licked every imaginable inch of this man's body. He responded to my touch as if it was a magnetic force. I enjoyed teasing him as much as I fantasized about pleasing him.

"Do you trust me?" I asked him as I circled my tongue around his navel.

"Until you give me a reason not too ... "

"That's exactly what I want to hear." I asked him to sit up as I placed a large bath towel on his sheet and pushed his oversize comforter to the floor.

"Go ahead and lay on the towel, stomach down. Listen to the music and let me relax you," I said to him as I swallowed the remainder of my wine. I adjusted the pillow beneath his head to ensure he was comfortable. I reached onto the table and placed the massage oil candle into my hand.

"This'll be warm, but it won't burn you," I warned him.

I gently blew out the flame, then dipped my finger into the oil to test the temperature. His body remained perfectly still as I poured the hot oil in a straight line down his back. Starting below his neck extending to his waistline, his arch keeping the oil centered. I massaged the oil into his soft skin, starting at his lower back, working my way up his spine, extending the pressure to his tense shoulders. Alternating between kneading and percussion techniques, I massaged every drop of oil into his skin until there was nothing left but silkiness.

The massage had his arousal at its heightened peak as he aggressively insisted he wanted to have me at that very moment. He reached one hand in the top drawer of his wooden dresser and grabbed a Magnum XL condom, tearing it open with his teeth. My sea parted for his grand entrance, anticipating its every inch of thickness. Paradise to say the

least, he was at a loss for words as his body became weakened t,
depths of my ocean.

"Are you fucking serious?" were his first words spoken.

My inner muscles squeezed and gripped him like a custom glove.
He handled me gently and slowly, loving my body down until we
were covered in sweat and couldn't take it anymore.

"Mmm mmm mmm …" he said shaking his head as I laid upon
his chest.

"What?" I responded.

"What am I going to do with you?" he asked as he pleasantly smiled.

I turned towards him and said, "I don't know, but please don't ever
stop doing what you're doing. I don't know what *this* is, but I like it."

"Same here, and that's what scares me the most," he said.

He kissed me on the forehead and we continued to lay, think, talk,
joke and laugh hysterically. He seemed like he was free with me, like he
really enjoyed these moments just being able to freely be who he was.

"Let me show you something," he said as he rolled over to grab his
phone, while I secretly admired his hairless derriere.

"I told you I don't care to see your Facebook or social media profiles,"
I said to him pouting.

He smiled and proceeded on his phone as he pulled me in close to
him. He opened his YouTube app and said, "You wanted to see me
play, right?"

I nodded in agreement as I watched him show me several videos of
him playing in front of unbelievably large crowds that went crazy to
his beats of perfection.

"That's amazing! You should feel accomplished and blessed."

"I am. You would love being on the road and going to my shows
overseas. I'd take you anywhere … anywhere, but to Brazil. No offense,
but the women there are just gorgeous, and I couldn't resist looking,
but I'd never disrespect you. You deserve to be with someone who's
loyal to you and doesn't take you for granted," he said as he kissed
my forehead.

25

"Okay. Be safe!" I called out to him, although I knew he wasn't the one in the morning bar type of guy.

He turned around towards me. He walked up so close on me that I could feel his heart beating.

"That's all you have to say? You did not spend any time with me on my fucking birthday. You got home from work a little after five, showered and dressed up to spend time with your *girls* as if that shit couldn't wait, and then you have the audacity to come in here after midnight, after the whole day has come and gone, thinking everything is supposed to be cool!"

He was right, and I was dead wrong, but my pride wouldn't let me go down without a fight. So, I opted to use my sharpest sword of all... the tongue. I fought fire with fire, attempting to make him out as the bad person so I wouldn't feel so shitty about what I did to him.

"First off, I didn't make plans until *you* decided to get your daughter without even a conversation with me, especially being you told me you haven't heard from her mammy in weeks. Plus, I know you're not talking. Let's not forget, I spent my 30th birthday alone. And since we're talking about special occasions, you got your 'side-piece' pregnant a few days before our fifth anniversary. You know the year you upgraded my wedding ring that you had presented by the chef at dinner, only to find out you gave *both* baby mama's duplicate phony rings only months later! Who does that?" I yelled at him in outrage.

"Why does everything have to always be about *you*? Why can you not leave the past in the past? That shit you just pulled was foul and you know it," he said furiously.

An alert sounded from my phone.

"Probably another damn email," I said innocently as I walked over to my purse that was on the bar stool. I picked my phone up and put it down immediately.

"Ha, I knew it!" I said as I put my phone back down. I lied.

My lock screen showed I had a text from Lenny inquiring if I were okay.

It was late and things were way too heated for me to boldly attempt to respond. I acted as if I was looking for some gum in my purse, even offered TJ an imaginary stick. I quickly sent Lenny a thumbs-up emoji, deleted the message thread, and put my phone on airplane mode, all while scrambling for fake gum.

The paranoia was real and living this double-life was way too exhausting. But it was the only thing that was making me feel alive again. I walked over to TJ.

"Look, I know you're upset so I'll spare you the apology as I know oh-too-well that sorry changes nothing. Plus, it's a new day and I too would love it if we could both learn to leave the past in the past. Sooo, let's celebrate daddy!" I said to him in an attempt to lighten his mood.

"It's late and everything is closing up," he said in a dry tone that I knew meant he didn't want to compromise and he didn't expect me to apologize since we both knew what I'd left to do.

"Wait! Let's go to the strip club and make it rain. My treat!" I said to him amused as I tugged on his arm, flashing a wad of ones I conveniently had on hand.

With minimal pleading, he agreed. We went to the strip club of his choice, this being our second time going together.

When we arrived, it was close to 2a.m. and the place was packed. Although it was closing in an hour, it was live! We sat upfront in the VIP section. We had drinks, mingled with the dancers and he received plenty of front row attention.

It was exciting to see him so turned on, as twisted as that may sound. But as the drinks were going down, the clothes were coming off and the only thing on my agenda was taking the heat off me and redirecting his focus.

The women there had beautiful faces and flawless figures. Their acts were XXX-rated to say the least. From the vaginal fireworks to crazy deep throat balloon tricks to the full, uncensored nudity. It felt good to see him smile, even if it was because of a fantasy that didn't star me.

While we were good for the moment, I knew the situation at hand remained the same. I knew that he was hurt, and I knew that it was because of me. Yet, I wasn't remorseful for my actions and that wasn't fair to him as my intention was never to get my feelings involved with another. I'm not sure if it was *who* I was becoming that scared me, or the fact that I was truly unsympathetic for my actions. I didn't trust myself and I'm a firm believer in karma. I have love and respect for the universe and its laws, but by the same token, I've always been on the receiving end of karma. So what did I really have to lose?

Chapter 3

THE BLISS

I'M FROM CHICAGO, born and raised primarily on the Southside. I grew up in an Islamic household in a family of five. I lived with both of my parents, along with my two sisters, me being in the middle. We never really had much and we moved around a lot as my dad never kept a stable job, or any job for that matter. I went to over thirteen different schools between K-12, never attending the same school for more than two grades and sometimes going to multiple schools in the same school year. Most people naturally assume my dad was in the military the way we moved around, but nope, he just couldn't hold down a job. It was hard for my mother to take care of three girls, a husband and the full weight of the household working minimal wage jobs. My daddy was never a fan of working for the "white man" as he called it. He would buy wholesale and set up shops here and there to sell his merchandise, but it was never enough to get or keep us out of the hole. At one time I even remember him opening a small retail shop in an Islamic owned shopping center in Markham, IL. He named his store JNR Williams…the first initials of me and my sister's names in birth order.

We were disciplined children and we appreciated the simplest things as we couldn't miss what we never had. We didn't celebrate holidays and we never had birthday parties. We saw a lot growing up and we went through a lot, yet always finding a way to make tasty lemonade from life's sour lemons. My dad instilled in us that what happened in our family stayed amongst our family and family was always first, no matter what. Family for us meant mama, daddy, and daughters … not healthy relationships with aunts, step-brothers, uncles, cousins, grandparents, and so forth. I was a daddy's girl and there wasn't anything that anyone could tell me about him to change my heart when I was a little girl, but then I grew up. My mother, on the other hand, is a very humble, loving and empathetic being. She has remained loyal to her character throughout all of life's storms thus far, even the most life-changing, unforgettable ones.

I will never forget the day that I watched my little sister die. We were living in Memphis, TN temporarily at the time. We were on our way to school and my mama proceeded through a caution light and was struck by a speeding car making a right turn. My sister was nine, I was eleven and my oldest sister was thirteen. My mother blamed herself and my daddy never offered her the reassurance she needed to psychologically heal. Daddy turned to alcohol and when he escaped to his drunken world, that would often lead to an episode of memory loss or amnesia the following day, we had to deal with the reality of what he did and said in those moments. He blamed my mother for his life's failures whenever he got drunk or mad, and brought up how she killed *their* daughter every chance he could, making her pay emotionally for the same accident over and over again.

I can only imagine the pain and guilt that she endured, as to lose a child is to lose a piece of your soul. I lost my first child at eight months pregnant, at the age of eighteen due to toxemia, and it was emotionally devastating. Eight months in the womb is incomparable to nine years on earth, but a mother's love for their child starts in the womb and that bond remains for life. It lives even when life ends.

I love both of my parents unconditionally, always seeking for ways to improve my relationship with them, but my dad, especially after the death of my sister, became hardcore, insensitive and untrustworthy. He had a very bad temper, especially when drunk, which was often. He lost all faith following her death and therefore he didn't instill the significance of religion in us beyond it.

It was hard to grow up and know that my mother wasn't happy, to see that she was choosing to settle because of us. She selflessly gave so much of her energy, her time and her faithful love. I honestly can't recall ever seeing it being reciprocated. I rarely saw my parents interact and they never showed each other genuine affection. I can't even remember them having one single date night. I didn't know exactly what love was, but I knew what it wasn't. I was always in love with the thought of being loved by someone as I knew how much I had the ability and natural desire to love within.

I remember the first time I fell for a boy and got my young heart broken. I remember the first time I gave a piece of my soul to another. I thought it was the end of the world when he walked away, but my world didn't end. It was then that I learned there is always someone wanting and willing to take the next person's place. It was then that I learned that there was magic in beauty, and to humbly be at the top of my class at all times was just icing on the cake. I was boy crazy and they were crazy about my pretty chocolate self in return. I thought the easiest way to get over someone old was to start something with someone new, and I did, and I got the same results every time.

Needless to say, tension on the home front didn't go away overnight from a few drinks and a strip-tease. I knew that it would take for me to fall back some from Lenny until I could figure out exactly what was occurring. I know that men play games all the time and I have a lot on the line if things go the wrong way. While my husband and I have no children together, he's been an integral part of my children's lives for many years. Their biological dad is a great provider. He is accomplished in his career, gets them bi-weekly consistently and definitely lives a lifestyle that provides for them efficiently. I'm blessed to have such a good relationship with him. We dated in high school and always vowed to put parenting first, regardless of our personal differences. We are the epitome of positive African-American co-parenting.

However, if it wasn't for my husband I truly can't imagine how difficult things would've been. Even now, I wouldn't even be able to get my children to and from school every day without his aid and support, especially with the recent changes in my schedule at work. Although it was summer break and their dad and I split summers in half, school was starting in less than two weeks and their time to come back home was approaching. I knew that I partially stayed for the wrong reasons, but it made my life make sense to me, especially now that the children are older and entering middle school. *I can do this for another five to seven more years,* I thought thinking ahead to senior year and graduations.

It had been two days since I last contacted Lenny. I knew with me getting off work so late it would be virtually impossible to see him again without causing suspicions. Lenny wasn't a "morning person" but he did sacrifice his sleep for me, as he called it. I went over to his place the next morning. He went back to sleep as soon as he let me inside.

After raiding his fridge and finding absolutely nothing, I made a quick trip to Kroger. When I returned he was still asleep. He slept for about another hour while I sat upright next to him reading a book.

"Why is waking up to you reading beside me so incredibly sexy?" he asked as he held my hand and kissed my wrist.

"Hungry?" I asked.

"I don't have any breakfast food downstairs."

"I already took care of that," I told him.

The other day he told me how his roommate doesn't eat pork and only buys stuff for *him* to eat. There was literally nothing in the fridge but random leftovers that I dared not open, let alone eat. He confessed that he loves thick cut bacon, and needless to say, I do too. So, I just ran with that.

I went downstairs and prepared a quick and simple breakfast then cleaned up the kitchen afterwards. Scrambled eggs with cheese, thick

apple-wood smoked bacon, toast, fresh sliced fruit and l
fresh strawberries. It was simple and delicious.

After our late breakfast he decided to finally start his day a
I stepped outside and called my job. I called-in sick. I didn
say anything to him about it as I didn't want it to seem tou creepy
or that I was doing it for him. I needed some time to put things into
perspective, and I knew with both him and TJ having to work, I'd
have adequate time to think things over. When I returned upstairs his
shower was ending. I took that time to straighten up some.

"Wait, did you clean my room up?" he asked smiling when he
realized the small difference.

"I just made up the bed and folded those few clothes on the chair,"
I said to him.

"I really need to go do laundry today," he said as he sniffed the shirt
he was getting ready to wear. We laughed in sync as he continued to
put his clothes on.

"So, will I see you tonight?" he asked.

"Only if you want to."

"Of course I want to, I always want to see you," he said. "I get off
at ten tonight but will probably leave early. What time are you getting
out of there?" he asked.

"Honestly, I called-in sick while you were in the shower and it has
nothing to do with you. I just have some things I need to take care
of," I said to him.

"Well that works out even better. I'm going to make us dinner
tonight. I'm going to make you the most amazing salmon and salad,
then pair it with some wine," he said reaching for a notepad as he had
several throughout his room.

He began to make his grocery list: *salmon, kale, spinach, quinoa,
bacon, gorgonzola, eggs, avocado, cucumbers, tomatoes.*

"Do you eat croutons?" he asked.

"I absolutely love them," I said.

"Me too, I literally sit in bed and eat them plain."

"Oh! Don't forget there is still bacon and eggs from earlier, so scratch those two," I reminded him.

He proceeded with the list: *croutons, honey roasted sunflower seeds, strawberry vinaigrette.*

"I'm so excited! You know what would really set the mood off tonight… a hookah. Come on, let's get out this house, get some air and go shopping," he said enthusiastically.

I grabbed my purse and we rode in his red Buick Enclave to a nearby hookah shop in the Mid-town area. We browsed their inventory and decided to go with a crystal blue dual-hose hookah. There were so many flavors of herbal molasses to choose from. We started off with three: vanilla, strawberry and mint.

I knew that it was getting close to my scheduled work time as TJ was starting to blow my phone up and the last thing I wanted was for him to call the office.

"So what's next?" I asked as we left the hookah shop.

"Time to shop for wine!" he said.

We headed to a very large liquor store with an astonishing wine selection.

"A dinner like that would pair well with a nice dry, red wine," he explained.

I told him that while I appreciated the 'education', I preferred a sweet subtle white wine. We compromised and got both an inexpensive bottle of Shiraz and a bottle of Yellow Tail Moscato. We agreed to just sip it after dinner.

"Do you need me to bring anything?" I asked.

He assured me that my presence alone was more than enough.

We went back to his place to try the hookah out. He assembled the hookah in no time, packing the ceramic bowl with molasses, then covering it with the screen. He lit the charcoal disc and it began to sizzle immediately as he held it in his hand using the provided metal tongue. He placed the coal atop and within minutes you could smell the tantalizing aroma.

He inhaled slightly from the metal tip of the hose, tasting the mint flavor for the first time.

"Yummy," he said as he invited me to give it a try. I choked from the inhalation, though I couldn't deny that it had a mildly sweet, delicious taste.

I stayed there and we smoked and chilled up until it was time for him to head out to work. I grabbed a couple of his belongings that needed to be washed as I had to do laundry myself when I got home anyway.

When I finally made it back to my house, I pulled up and immediately noticed that the lawn was perfectly manicured and the garbage and recycling bins were pulled to the street for tomorrow's pick up.

I went inside and I found all of TJ's closets and drawers empty along with a note on the crisp linen bedding: "You Win. I'm done," was all that the note said.

I called TJ several times and he sent my calls straight to voicemail. After ignoring several back-to-back calls from me, he finally sent me a text message: "Called your job to make sure you were okay and they told me you were sick. I felt like shit once again. You're obviously where you want to be. Have fun."

I could've easily gone back and forth with him, but the situation still remained the same. I left it at that, not making any further comments or asking any additional questions. I proceeded to prepare myself for the night's adventure.

I got the small load of laundry out of the way, even though I knew I had several hours to spare. My initial plan was to come home and come to some sort of an understanding with TJ, but I was in no mood for drama or lying. For the first time in a very long time I felt happy, and happy doesn't usually last long for me. So, I cherished and nourished it. I grabbed a notebook and a pen and proceeded to express my thoughts...

equal is what you were foreseen to be.
understanding its enigmatic complexity.
our intelligence is beyond what lies at the surface.
Never underestimating your predetermined purpose.
Your presence stimulates desires within.
When I close my eyes, I can feel your touch against my skin.
You are the breath of fresh air once the storm has passed by.
Reminding me that life is too short to live a lie.
Your perfection excites me.
Your beauty delights me.
Kisses so passionate, my waters overflow.
Clinging to your sheets as my body loses control.
Grasping my thighs as I pull on your hair.
Moaning so loud that the neighbors can hear.
Wanting you to beat it up, then go back down and eat it up.
Tasting your love, so thick and strong.
Craving you in me all night long.
I think about you more often than I should.
I dream about you as someone in love would.
You calm the turbulence in my life.
Taking me away from negativity and strife.
I just want to say thank you for opening up to me.
In a world filled with deception it gets hard to really see.
Nevertheless, I'm blessed for whatever this may be.

I wasn't sure how the ambiance would be, so I prepared and packed an orchid color Victoria's Secret's lace negligee along with my multi-speed water proof LED bullet vibrator. I revised my poetic rough draft and thought it'd only be fair to share my thoughts with Lenny as he was the inspiration behind the rhymes.

I freshened up, fed the dog and headed out to east Memphis.

I went to the nearby IMAX cinema to purchase a ticket for a movie playing at 10:05pm. Though I had no intention of actually watching the movie, I just needed to use it as my alibi since I knew I'd have to lie. I wasn't ready to face my truth. I wasn't ready to acknowledge that hurt. Acknowledging it makes it real.

I contacted Lenny to let him know that I was in the vicinity and to just let me know when he was ready. To my surprise he ended his workday much earlier than I anticipated to get a jump start on the evening, assuring me I could head his way whenever my heart desired to.

I was definitely ready. I tore off the admit portion of the ticket and threw it in the parking lot of the theater. I tossed the remaining ticket stub and receipt for 'one adult admission' onto the passenger seat as I pulled off.

"Mmmm…it smells amazing," I said as I walked into his home.

"Do you want to eat now or wait?" he asked.

"I'm starving babe."

"Great! I'm almost finished with dinner," he said as he kissed me on the cheek and scurried back to his pan-seared salmon fillets.

"I'll meet you upstairs in a few, the hookah is already going," he called out from the kitchen.

When I got upstairs he had "The Notebook" playing and a big soft pallet made of pillows and blankets in front of his bed on the floor. The hookah was set up on his bedside table, which he placed beside the pallet.

"Yummy," I said as I tasted the strawberry flavor that he'd chosen.

I undressed into my negligee and sat on the pallet awaiting his presence. I could hear his footsteps as he came into the room.

"Very very sexy," he said as he walked into the room admiring my lingerie.

The plates were beautifully prepared. I thanked him for all the work that he put into everything. I tasted a piece of the salmon chopped amidst the salad. It was cooked to perfection, with a crisp char finish.

It was all just a dream. Stuff like that didn't happen to girls like me in "real life". We sat down and ate together, then followed it with chilled red wine for him and white wine for myself.

After dinner, we continued to sip wine and smoke from the hookah.

"Come on," he said as he reached for my hand. He led me to the bed. I synced my Pandora premium to his Bluetooth speaker.

"I already have a charger plugged in on the other side of the bed ready for you," he said right as I was going to ask him for his charger.

"You are so freakin' awesome!" I told him as I pulled him onto the bed and sat in an upright position on him.

"You shouldn't be nervous around me anymore," he said smiling as he made a reference to me being *helpless* during our last encounter.

"You do realize that I've never allowed nor trusted anyone to take control of my body in the manner in which I allow you too," I said to him.

I'm not sure where his head or heart was when it came down to us, but the only thing I do know is that I can't take another heart break.

"So how long do I have you tonight?" he asked.

"As long as you want me to be here," I said to him naughtily.

"Don't say that to me. I want you to stay every time you come over and you know it. I hate that I can't hold you in my arms all night long and wake up to you still in my arms in the morning," he said to me as he gently pulled my face towards his and kissed my lips.

I was falling for this man deeply and quickly, and it scared me. I felt awakened when I was with him. He made me feel foolish for not following my heart and fulfilling my dreams. He supported my writing and my candle making without making me feel like my goals were unattainable. He encouraged me and made me feel like there was a better life beyond my chosen path of misery. Maybe I was misinterpreting him. Maybe I was being delusional.

I dreaded the thought of fear and rejection, so I've lived life in the comfort lane and while it hasn't gotten me as far as I envisioned, it has kept me safe, or so I thought. There was so much hatred, resentment and bitterness within me from my chosen hand that I felt cursed with the inability to love, and it was happening right before my eyes, out of the blue. It could all be a mirage and me just looking too deeply or wanting too badly for it to be real, but I knew it was real because I felt it. Just as I felt the pain from the deception, I felt the love and it was always a pleasure to show my appreciation.

That night after we made love I lay on his chest and we talked for hours. He looked to the future while I simply cherished the moment we were in.

"I know it's crazy and this is moving really fast but … I love you. I'm not asking you to say it back to me right now because I only want you to say it when you feel it, but I love you. I really do. I told my roommate and he said that he knows and to just be careful with you…"

"I know that considering circumstances it's probably hard for you to believe, but I'm very loyal and when I love, I love hard and I go hard. I still don't know exactly what *this* is, but I love you too," I said to him.

The awkward silence that followed was abruptly interrupted by loud music and hysterical laughter. He jumped up furiously, expeditiously putting on his basketball shorts along with an oversize jersey and stormed out of the room. I used that time to freshen up with my feminine wipes and adjust myself in his mirror. I made the bed as I sang aloud and in sync to India Arie's "Ready for Love". After that song ended so did another, and another, and he'd still not come back upstairs. I started to worry until I heard footsteps.

I quickly propped myself up in the bed as if I never moved. The door opened, but it wasn't him. It was his roommate's girlfriend. *Is this bitch lost?* I thought. I immediately snatched the shaggy throw at the end of the bed and wrapped it around me.

"Hey! I didn't mean to scare you. I know we haven't properly met but I'm Ne-ne. I just wanted to speak and check on you since the boys left *us* up here by ourselves," she said to me laughing.

Dressed in oversized, baggy clothes, Ne-ne had a brown sugar skin tone, was 5'2", and about 115lbs with very short hair.

and uncomfortable at the same time. She continued to talk and I just nodded occasionally, agreeing here and there. I removed the throw from around my shoulders and wrapped it around my waist, so I could lie back down. I laid on my stomach, closed my eyes and bobbed my head to the beat, hoping she'd get the picture and get lost. She continued talking and I could hear her voice coming closer and closer towards me. She asked me if smoke bothered me and if I had a lighter. I rolled over to grab a lighter out of my purse and I felt a finger poke my ass. I turned around quickly.

"I just wanted to see if it felt as soft as it looks," she giggled.

I stared her down as I handed her the lighter.

"Everything good?" asked a masculine voice. I was relieved to see Lenny back.

"Catch you around big bro!" Ne-ne said to Lenny as she walked out of the room grinning and patting him on the shoulder.

"Did she try something with you?" he asked as he drank a Miller High-life beer.

"Why would you automatically assume she'd try something with me? What type of woman do you think I am?" I asked defensively.

"No, no, no, I just know Ne-ne and she can get pretty wild. You think I'm a beast down there...," he said laughing and shaking his head. I didn't see any humor in the situation.

"So, you're speaking from personal experience I take it?" I inquired.

"Yes, but not like that," he responded.

I felt the bullshit coming, but I respected his truth. It happened before me and had nothing to do with me.

"How do you feel?" he asked.

"A little tired but I'm okay. I still have a couple hours to hang. I gave myself a 3a.m. curfew. Don't want to get too comfortable in your space," I said laughing.

"I have a pill if you want to take half of it … I mean it'll keep you up so you won't fall asleep," he said.

Not knowing that it was an ecstasy pill, or questioning what it was, I nodded in agreement. He got me a glass of cold water. He placed the pill between my front teeth and told me to bite down on it. When I bit the pill, I bit more than half of it. More like seventy-five percent of it.

"Oh my god! I'm so sorry!" I said to him.

He laughed and assured me that it was no big deal as he'd just taken a whole pill downstairs. He finished the remainder of what I didn't consume and downed it with a swish of E&J liquor.

"I have a confession. I'm a big kid. Can we watch Batman vs. Superman?" he asked.

It was the cutest thing ever to me. Besides, I figured out he was a "big kid" long ago when I saw his love and obsession for Batman. It's creepy, yet sexy at the same time.

"I'd love to watch it!" I said to him, although I was a Superman fan and not at all shy about making declarations and defending my hero.

My body was extremely cold as I touched his skin with my icy fingertips. I sent a chill down his spine.

"You must be anemic?" he asked.

"Actually, I am and drinking anything cold only makes it worse," I said to him.

The room was of average temperature but my body was quivering. He pulled my body close to his, so I could warm up quickly.

"Lay on top of me, I'll warm up faster," I told him. He looked at me as if I was making it up just because I wanted him on top.

Well, if that's what he thought then *Ding! Ding! Ding!* he was absolutely right. He got on top of me and I wrapped my long chocolate legs around his waist. He was the cream filling of my Oreo and I couldn't get enough.

I traced my face with his fingers then placed his index finger in my mouth. I sucked his finger playfully, then forcefully. I could feel him getting aroused as I ground my pelvis against his.

"We used the last condom earlier," he said in between kisses.

"We don't need a condom to kiss," I whispered into his ear, nibbling on his lobe.

I reached underneath the pillow and grabbed my bullet vibrator, which was purposely placed there. I slid it between my thighs and massaged myself through my panties. He could feel the vibrations against his testicles. He slid his hand between my legs, removed the vibrator from my hand and took over pleasing me. I could hear his fingers swishing around inside of my body from the wetness.

He licked my juices off his fingers and said, "Fuck it."

He moved my panties to the side and entered my body slowly and deeply. I felt all of him in all of me and I unassumingly enjoyed his adulation. I could tell from his initial *exhale* that it was a sigh of relief. My girl was tight and right.

"This is too good. This is crazy good," he said as he found his natural rhythm of perfection.

"Turn around, Imma cum too fast like this," he said as he quickly tossed my body over.

I positioned myself to take him in without constraint. I threw it back like I was auditioning for the next Juvenile "Back That Ass Up" video. I could feel the drugs moving through my veins as I rode him like I was performing at an endless rodeo. We made love to the sound of our own beats. The sounds created by personal moments of ecstasy and pleasure, by moments that didn't belong to us.

"I love you."

"I love you too."

Chapter 4

THE CHANGE

"**U**GH … I don't want to leave babe."
I whined as I looked at the clock and laid on his chest. It was after 3a.m. but I knew I had the house to myself so I had no real sense of urgency.

"If it were up to me your ass wouldn't be going anywhere, but I understand. As a matter of fact, no, I don't understand. What's so complicated considering what he did to you and the fact that you two don't have any kids together? Never mind … I'm good," he said to me.

I didn't know if I should feel flattered or just confused. It was almost as if he just instantly shut down.

"I promise you that I'm doing everything on my end to expedite this. This is a process and I promise you that I'd never play games with your heart," I told him.

"I swear if you hurt me, I would never… No, it would take me a very long time to *ever* trust another woman," he said, putting emphasis on *ever*.

"Look at me, you will *never* have to worry about me hurting you. I would never put you in a predicament like that. If he and I were really on good terms, trying to save our marriage, why would I be at your house at 3a.m.? I'm a woman. What man would allow his *wife* to be out that late without an APB being issued? The respect left a long time ago. I'm so sorry that things are the way that they are, but I'm just as in love with you and as equally scared to say the least, whether you believe it or not," I said to him.

"I don't even know what *this* is. I went to a party with my sister the other day and a few of her friends were trying to get with me and I honestly told them that I was good. Not only did it shock my sister to hear me say that, but I mean it shocked me too, especially considering these circumstances. I love you. I really do," he said.

We sighed deeply and in sync.

"Mmm…mmm…mmm" he said shaking his head as he kissed me on the forehead. I loved him too and I could feel the love that he had for me, and it felt good to love and be loved in return.

I took the long way home that night as I knew with school starting within a week I had to make some major decisions. I made it home right before 4am. I was startled to see TJ's truck parked in the driveway. I powered my phone down completely before I got out my truck.

When I opened the door the house smelled of fresh lemon Pine-Sol. The house was spotless and there he was in the bedroom sitting on top of the comforter of the perfectly made bed playing a game on his phone while watching a Netflix movie on the big screen. He didn't say a word to me and I didn't say one either. I dressed into my night clothes, grabbed a pillow off the bed, and proceeded to the couch in the living room. I cut the lights out and curled up in my daughter's blanket at the end of the leather sofa. I powered my phone back on and listened to ocean waves at a low volume to put me to sleep before the sun came up.

The living room light came on.

"So you tired? No, get up!" TJ said as he slung my legs from the couch onto the floor.

He pulled my arm and snatched me off the couch, dropping my phone. A new message came in and I knew it was Lenny making sure I was safe. We both immediately looked at the phone which lay

face down on the hardwood floor. I was praying that the gla.
cracked from the impact.

"Why are you doing this?" I asked him as I hurried to grab my ⸏ ⸏.

"Why am I doing this? It's 4 o'clock in the fucking morning and
you're asking me why *I'm* doing this? Yeah, why am *I* doing this? I
came back thinking we could talk things over and I waited like a damn
fool when again you were where you wanted to be. I called you over
twenty times. Your voicemail is now full. Why are *you* doing this?"
he said to me.

My head was bowed as tears streamed down my face. I lifted my
teary face to meet his eyes.

"I can't stop," I said to him.

Tears fell from his eyes. My body was numb. He cut the light off
and walked back into the bedroom. Within a blink of an eye, he
kissed me on the cheek, handed me his wedding band, house keys
and walked out the door.

"I'll be leaving for Atlanta next week. You can take me off the car
insurance and phone plan," he added as he walked out the door and
asked me to lock up *my* house behind him.

A part of me felt set free, while another part of me was dying as I
knew that I hurt someone who I knew had love for me. I've never been
in a situation like this and I never thought I'd ever be in this situation,
but I knew I wasn't happy being married to someone I couldn't trust
and wasn't in love with.

I didn't have the energy or strength to argue with TJ, nor the desire
to stop him from walking out that door as I've done so many times
before. I slept alone in the house with the exception of our expecting
Shih Tzu who lay at the foot of the bed. I listened to all of the sounds
of the night while my thoughts ran endless miles. I heard a series of
loud noises in the attic, but was too afraid to move. I was scared and
I deserved to be. I knew I was letting go of the biggest part of me for
something that's not guaranteed. It wasn't the *known* that petrified
me, but the *unknown*.

With TJ being gone, I had to take on additional roles to say the least. I guess I didn't realize how much he did until he left. I admit that he's been the more "hands-on" parent over the years as I've always worked crazy unpredictable shifts. Because of his *troubled* past, self-employment was a winning solution as he'd never truly make what his work ethics were worth.

TJ is often described as a "jack of all trades", so he knew how to keep money steady and make things happen when needed. I couldn't stand the thought of having to ask Jordan to keep the kids for another school year, as he did for the second half of their school year during my initial breakdown in 2015. However, I didn't know any other way to make it work as my schedule was consistent, but inconvenient to anyone with children.

I hit Jordan up and asked to meet with him urgently and he agreed. Jordan and I dated our senior year of high school, and then he went off to join the military directly afterwards. Once he finished base training, he and his new fiancé moved to Washington where he was stationed. Shortly after, he sadly learned that the little girl he thought he fathered was not his as paternity tests revealed, getting his new marriage annulled as a result of the deception. I too was wounded from a disappointing relationship that left me as a single parent. It was then when we rekindled our high school romance.

I flew to Seattle, WA with my five-month old daughter at the time to be with him after I completed my second semester at the University of Memphis. My family urged me not to go as I was making a big mistake and would be back, but it's hard to understand that when you're twenty years old, you think you're in love, and you think you know everything. He shipped all my belongings to his home in Oak Harbor, WA and they made it there before we did. I loved Washington and I embraced my new life. I got pregnant with our first child there and two years later, I got pregnant with a set of twins, a boy and girl. He has always been good to the kids and they have never needed for anything.

I drove to his newly built home in Olive Branch. Without hesitation, he agreed to keep the kids.

"Are you sure this is what you want to do?" he asked.

"No, but options are limited and time is of the essence. The new school year is just days away in DeSoto County where you live, and the kids need to get adjusted to the change. I don't know what else to do with TJ being gone," I said to him desperately.

"So, what happened? Another baby?" he joked.

"Ha-ha. NO! I just have major trust issues and it's not fair to neither of us. He doesn't want to let go and I can't keep holding on knowing that the trust is gone," I said.

"Yeah, that was a really big pill to swallow, but the kids should never be your reason for staying because I will always be here for them."

"I know, and I appreciate you for all that you do. Thank you."

Over the course of the next week, Lenny and I spent time together every day that our schedules permitted without inconvenience. Every visit was like a one-way trip to euphoria, regardless to if we sexed, popped pills for the thrill, watched random movies, or just talked and chilled. I became more comfortable around his closest friends and even had an opportunity to meet his only sibling one evening. My vibe was that his sister, a beautiful NBA cheerleader, wasn't favorable of me because of the "circumstances". He, on the other hand, insisted that he knows her well and she actually liked me very much. He claimed that if she didn't like me then I'd know without a doubt, but I was always weary of the shame behind my name.

At times I just couldn't see where I fit into his world. I knew that he one day wanted to settle down as he expressed on several occasions. He wanted to start a family of his own as he had no children. We even discussed surgically getting my tubes untied if we got to that point as they were tied after my pregnancy with the twins. I vowed to get them untied if and only if I met a man with no children or only one child. Then, we would have to be married and financially stable … then and only then would I sacrifice and bare him *one* child.

I know that dating a woman with children is challenging, although my kids are well taken care of and in no need of a father figure. Furthermore, add a painful failed marriage to the mix. I knew I was putting a heavy load on him. I just hope he knew that my heart was sincere.

As the week came to an end, I was beginning to feel emotionally and mentally overwhelmed. Friday night when I picked up the kids, my daughter was so ecstatic about making the band in middle school. She told me that she now wanted to be a percussionist, alongside an aspiring veterinarian. Her love for musical instruments was new to me. She has always had a love for music as she studies and takes dance, but I never imagined her having the desire to play an actual instrument. I supported her one hundred percent as any parent would, thinking ahead to potential scholarships. Besides, I'd be lying if I said I wasn't even happier that she chose the snare drums to play. I admit that I may have persuaded her just a tad bit, but she was thrilled when I told her I would let her meet a professional drummer who could possibly give her some beginner tips.

"So, if you're really serious about playing the drums, I'll see if my *friend* can give you some pointers. He plays the drums professionally and he's not that bad on the eye either," I said to her smiling as I winked at her through the rearview mirror.

"Ma, I hope you're not talking about Robert," she said.

I almost choked at the thought of that name. Robert was a blunder from my past, and I have very few experiences that I truly wish could be erased from my memory.

Robert was the drummer at his family's small church. He was seven years younger than me, charismatic, comedic, and just ridiculously handsome. He and I worked together during the time my marriage fell apart in late 2015. My leave of absence at work caused major speculation and I knew I had to put the rumors to rest by resurfacing.

Robert was the first person I saw when I returned to work. He didn't ask any questions, he simply approached me and said, "You don't know

50

how much *I've* missed you while you were gone." He then genuinely asked for a hug. I hugged him and while I knew the embrace was a potential HR violation, being I was his supervisor, it felt so damn good … it was like my body was doing an internal exhale. I'd never thought twice about him in the past as I was faithful to my husband, plus I'd already heard a fair share of rumors about him. Not to mention, I wasn't into "light-skinned" brothas, him being my first.

During that time, I was emotionally weak and susceptible from the affair, and Robert preyed upon my vulnerability like a thief in the night waiting for the right time to slip his way inside. Robert told me what I needed to hear to selfishly get what he wanted out of me. He falsely confided in me that his babymama had thrown him out on the streets with just the clothes on his back and he'd been sleeping in his cousin's vehicle and crashing with friends because *she* was caught cheating.

All of our mutual friends warned me to stay away from him. They said he was trouble looking for a thrill but he convinced me that they were just jealous of what we had, and I foolishly believed him. Robert and I grew closer and I quickly moved him into my spare room inside the garage since it was the dead of winter, and I can't lie and say that I enjoyed being in that house alone.

After being there for only a few short weeks, he asked my kids for their permission to take me out on a date and they were overjoyed. He was young, twenty-three at the time, so they considered him fun and a friend. He treated my daughters like princesses'.

Things were going great until people at work began to question our transparent closeness. It wasn't long before the secret was out, and when that secret came out, so did all of the others.

Shortly after our affair was exposed, I found out that Robert was very married and still pursuing his wife, whom I was led to believe was *just* the mother of his child. That woman harassed me endlessly, and I knew that she was entitled just because of her title.

I turned to marijuana and extreme alcoholism. Being drunk and high was the only way I felt numb. I found out that he was on probation for a pending drug charge, so while he couldn't smoke marijuana because it was hard to get out of his system, he had a costly and addictive cocaine and pill habit. Unfortunately, I was his source of financial aid for it. Every Friday when we got paid, he had his hand out like one of my children looking for allowance. I can remember waking up one morning in the wee hours to find him at my kitchen table with his homeboys playing cards, snorting cocaine, as if my kids weren't just a few feet away.

Alongside being married, Robert had sex with another woman in my home while I was at work. She showed up at my house asking for my "brother", describing my home from top to bottom. When confronted he became physically abusive, punching me over and over while I did nothing but cry and take the blows. That was the first time I was hit. Who I was becoming scared me as I never had to hide physical pain with TJ.

Nevertheless, the final straw was when he got his wife pregnant while we were *supposed* to be together, as she sent me a screenshot of her announcing the news to him. He responded that he was so happy for their new blessing and really wanted their marriage to work. I refused to compete with another baby. It's like he took all the bad shit I told him TJ did to me and put me through it all over again, only this time at an accelerated pace.

I played the role as long as I could, continuously allowing Robert to go back and forth between his wife and me. Continuously giving him what he didn't deserve, all out of hurt and spite. I admit that it initially felt good being the one to finally tell another woman, "Your marriage means nothing to me" and "Your man is *our* man," as I was always the one who was told those words.

However, when I learned who she really was, it began to hurt me to know that I was hurting her as all she wanted me to do was stop interfering. I knew how that felt. I could sense from the conversations and confrontations she and I had that she was a good mother and a good wife to his unworthy ass. He fought her while she carried his unborn child, so I knew he couldn't possibly respect me … or women. She didn't deserve that, and while I knew I wasn't the first and surely wouldn't be the last, I didn't want to be a contributing factor anymore. Her pregnancy became my way out.

I wrote her many apologetic letters but never had the courage to mail any of them. I guess it's true when people say, 'hurt people like to hurt people'. While I may forget her face and her name over time, I'm certain that she will never forget me as I was at the root of her hurt.

The whole situation was a deceitful nightmare, ending before it ever began. Needless to say, going back to TJ was the only thing that I knew to do, as he was my shelter from the rain, even if he caused the storm.

The weekend with the kids flew by as they always seem to do, and I was dreading the start of a new week. Work was becoming more and more stressful with the increases in production. Money was at an all-time low as TJ left me in a bind with a major mutual bill, but I knew that it was only out of hurt. I began to feel down in spirit and as my flesh weakened, the only way I knew how to feel anything was to be with Lenny as it was always a constant rush.

My late nights turned into full overnight stays with no regrets. I would get off work and go straight to his place and then leave the following morning. Some mornings I would cook, other mornings we would just sleep in until one of us had something to do. My adrenaline was at an unsurpassed high and he was addictive. The only thing I did at my home was feed the pets, shower daily and pack my clothes for whatever journey the new night would bring.

Lenny's birthday was quickly approaching, a little over a week away. He asked me if I'd spend his birthday with him at the Peabody Hotel. Of course I was ecstatic and said "Yes!"

Coincidentally his birthday fell on a Thursday, my day off, as the work schedule is posted a month in advance. That worked out perfect being it was too short notice to request off. I scheduled my hair appointment in advance for early the morning of his birthday. I anticipated perhaps taking him to brunch to kick off his day, then let him go his way and catching up with him later that evening. That was *my* ideal plan.

I was apprehensive about buying him a gift as I didn't want to come off too serious, too strong, too soon and scare him away, but I valued his presence in my life and I wanted to express it through a small token of my appreciation. I ordered him a set of personalized drumsticks with his name engraved on one drumstick and an inspirational quote from a tattoo on his arm engraved on the other drumstick.

Additionally, I got him a corresponding composing notebook as he composes music, along with several other personable items, including a Batman shirt and collectors watch to add to his collection. Nothing over the top, just a little gesture of my sincere appreciation. I was honestly undecided on what to get and felt that each gift represented something different, so I got each of them.

Nevertheless, the clouds began to roll in slowly, though I chose to ignore the obvious. Immediate text responses turned into three-to-four hour delays, if any reply at all. The Sunday before his birthday he had a big gig to prepare for. I was skeptical about agreeing to come over as he agreed to hang out the previous night. I drove across town to his home and my knocks and calls went unanswered for almost fifteen minutes. I knocked so hard and so long that the glass of the window shook. At one point I thought the neighbors nearby would call the police on me and I was in no mood to argue with or lie to MPD. I felt crazy, deranged and foolish. I left and didn't hear from him until late afternoon the next day. It was then when we decided to try again for that night. He definitely had me feeling some type of way, and I was in no mood for another blank trip as gas prices steadily rose.

Lenny was apologetic when I arrived as he said it was unintentional.

"Baby, you know that I sleep hard and I don't want you to feel like I don't want you over here because I do. Trust me, you wouldn't be here if I didn't want you here. Earlier today I told my roommate that if you ever knock on the door and I'm asleep to just let you in and you can just let yourself in my room. I don't have anything to hide.

Now, I do have to get some practice in tonight, but I promise you that it won't take too long. I can listen to almost any song and learn it by heart in less than thirty minutes without ever reading the music," he said to me.

I reassured him that working on his music was not and would never be a problem. The last thing that I wanted to do was be a burden or impose as I respect personal space. He put on his wireless beats, closed his eyes and begin to listen to the beat of the music. He was flickering his drumsticks so fast in the air that I could hear the air gusts. I swear I thought I was going to catch a whiplash if I didn't get some additional clearance. I played brain games on my phone until he finished. While it took a little longer than he anticipated, I enjoyed every minute. You could see his passion and love for what he does, and as a writer, I understand and respect the art of it.

That night we just laid together and talked. He was his usual tipsy and sex was becoming obsolete as this was the third consecutive visit without it. I couldn't stay all night as we both had obligations the following morning. Everything was weighing so heavily on my mind and it was written all over my face. He encouraged me to open up and talk to him about what was on my mind as he reassured me that he wouldn't judge. At my request, he gave me another pill, then another. I opened up about my past and the things that hurt me the most. He was receptive and respected what I had to say.

He reassured me that nothing would change, and everything would be okay, but after that everything changed.

Nothing was ever the same again …

Chapter 5

THE REALITY

I WENT OVER TO his house the following Tuesday, just two days before his birthday. I was cramping and not in the best of mood, but still we laid and talked all night. It seemed like his mind was all over the place, jumping from one random subject to the next, but I listened attentively as he's done for me on numerous occasions. I blamed it on the cocaine that he didn't know I already knew about. Besides, with his birthday only a couple of days away, I didn't want to press the issue being pessimistic. The next morning, I left early as he said he had to do laundry and take care of some business before work. Despite him telling me that everything was "good" between us, I could feel the distance and the walls being built.

His birthday finally arrived, and while I didn't hear from him much, I still went ahead as planned as he hadn't said otherwise. We texted once during the morning as I was in motion early. He didn't say much, other than he was working for a few hours. I went to my hairdresser, Dee, who not only specializes in natural hair, but she's also one of my besties.

Dee braided my thick, natural hair down and did me a sew-in with my twenty-inch Brazilian wavy hair. I figured maybe it was time to change up my look as I didn't want to bore him. Dee is also my unofficial part-time therapist. We talk about the good, the bad, the ugly, and all of the gossip in between.

I didn't hear from Lenny at all during the three hours it took to get my hair done. I was starting to get nervous as I knew he got off several hours ago and the day was fading away.

My texts messages went unanswered and my calls were sent straight to voicemail. I tried my best to space them apart as I didn't want to ruin whatever mood he was in.

I could feel a tightness in my chest but I continued to try to reach him. You know that feeling you get when you *hope* that something is wrong, but in reality, you already *know* the person is out doing wrong, yet you desperately seek confirmation that will change nothing upon discovery.

I proceeded to get dressed and did my make-up as if I was still going out with him. I grabbed his gift and headed to his place only to find that there was no one at his home. I stopped by his job and was informed that he'd left for the day. I irrationally wondered if he was already at the hotel waiting on me, but I didn't have his room number, so I knew that wasn't the case.

There were so many mixed feelings and emotions brewing within. I sent him a text:

"I'm not sure what's going on. I thought we'd spend time together at some point today, but I'll be dropping your gift off in 30 minutes. If you're still not home, your gift will be on your porch. Take care."

He didn't respond even though I knew in my heart he saw the message. I kept my end of the deal and headed back to his place to drop off the gift bag. When I returned, his truck was still gone but I'm almost 99.9% sure that I saw his sister's white Mercedes backing up to his house.

I saw her brake lights from a half a mile away. She kept her foot on the brakes for at least sixty seconds. There is rarely traffic on his street, which is presumably why she didn't get rear ended for being in the street that long.

I assumed at that point she was reaching out to him to say either she was leaving or just getting here. Either way, I was appalled that he didn't have to decency to at least accept his gift himself.

Like who has to force someone to accept a gift? It's not like he didn't know. I asked him if he wanted his gift when it was first delivered, but he said that he wanted to wait until his actual birthday to receive his gifts.

There is no doubt in my mind that he sent her over there to pick it up. I decided to keep the gift bag in my truck as I sped past her car. I'm certain that she saw me too as my truck has signature decals on it.

The next day I had to be at work early and my shift flew by. I had very little time to focus on my own worries as I was overwhelmed with my work flow. I checked my phone periodically out of the day in hopes he would come around, but not a single text or call. I even contemplated throwing the gifts away as I stared the gift bag down through my rearview mirror while I ate my lunch in my truck. I could feel the end coming and the very thought of it made me sick to my stomach. My home was destroyed and I was losing the one I trusted my heart with the most.

When my shift ended, I sat in my truck smoking, debating on whether or not I should just pop up over his house. I am definitely not the type of chick to just pop up on a man, but I've never been in a situation where I was genuinely concerned about someone and didn't know if they were okay. I gulped down the hot Red Bull in my cup holder and proceeded to his place of residence. The only thing that I knew is he talked about his birthday nonstop leading up to it and went M.I.A. on *me* the day of. I can always remember TJ telling me that I always assume the worst and needless to say, that is the truth.

When I arrived to Lenny's house I saw his Enclave parked in its usual spot. I felt a sigh of immediate relief. There were balloon ribbons hanging from the bottom of his rear driver door. His windows were tinted, but you could clearly see the after math of his special day from his vehicle alone. I was relieved that he was okay and while a part of nted to just drop the gift off and give him time to come around, a part of me wanted to know … needed to know.

I proceeded to his door and knocked. I knocked over and over again. I called his phone and it rang steadily, whereas yesterday I was deliberately forwarded to his voicemail. *Maybe I should just leave the gift bag on his windshield*, I thought.

I could see the tall, husky shadow of his roommate in the kitchen as the curtains were thin. I knocked harder but still no answer. I sat in my truck and sent him a long text message before I pulled off. I was so done at that moment…

"Look, I'm not sure what's going on or what I did to you for you to just completely shut me out, but what you're doing is hurting me and I know that you know this. I was honestly worried about you, but I see now that you're okay as I came to check on you and drop your gift off. People make time for the things and people that are important to them. I now know where I stand. You don't have to worry about me reaching out to you beyond this conversation. Take care and see you around".

When I pulled off I felt accomplished and victorious. I listened to my favorite "man-hater" R&B songs by Keyshia Cole and K. Michelle as I took the scenic route home. I was hurt and I told myself over and over again that everything was okay and I wasn't going to cry. I could feel the tears rolling down my cheeks. I put my sunglasses on to hide the pain in my eyes. I drove for hours until I couldn't see the lanes anymore as my tears continuously streamed. I turned onto a quiet street in Tunica, MS where I parked my truck and lowly listened to depressing old school R&B music, kicking it off with Bobby Womack.

The next night I was invited to attend a 30th birthday bash for a close girlfriend of mine at a night club in east Memphis. I called her to cancel but she insisted that I go as it'd be refreshing to escape my reality … besides you can only have one 'Dirty Thirty' party, right?

I agreed and in the midst of getting ready I received my first text from Lenny since his absence urging me that we needed to talk seriously.

My heart dropped but I was determined to enjoy myself and remain in control. I responded that I was actually going to a friend's party but would be more than happy to drop his gift off if he was available. It sickened me to force him to accept it. He agreed and I made sure that I looked flawless.

When I arrived at his house I parked on the street instead of under the carport as I normally would. When I made it to the door, I notified him that I was outside. I was terrified of what was to come but I mentally prepared myself for the worse as his sudden change in behavior signaled another romance escalating. I was hoping that he'd want to talk about whatever it was right now while I had my confidence high and my guards up. I wanted nothing more than a legitimate and understanding excuse to not make the party, and what's more understanding than a broken heart?

I'm not quite sure what came over me, but as soon as he opened the door I handed him the gift bag and proceeded to walk away. I could hear the door close as I walked away. *This hot yellow negro had me so messed up*! I turned back around and knocked on the door. He came back to the door looking like a deer caught in the headlight.

"Really?" I asked him.

He shrugged his shoulders in a nonchalant manner with a toothpick hanging from his teeth and said, "Well, you walked off…".

While his observation was accurate, I did not get the reaction I hoped for, so I lied, which was something I *never* had to do with him.

"I thought you were coming outside behind me since you knew I wasn't staying. Besides, I didn't expect an invite in after these last few days," I said to him.

He didn't confirm or deny anything. There was an awkward silence. I felt like I was standing in front of a monstrous stranger trapped inside his body.

"Well, I won't take up your night, besides I have to get going anyway," I hesitantly said to Lenny.

"Hold this, Imma grab my shoes," he said to me as he handed me the gift bag back and proceeded to slide his feet into a pair of shoes near the doorway. I saw his roommate walk past the doorway and instead of being his usual self, welcoming of my presence, he gave me a cold-hearted gangster nod.

His look sent chills down my spine.

When Lenny stepped outside he told me that he had to play early the following morning but promised we would talk the next night. I asked him to wait until I left before he opened the gift.

On my way to the club I got a call from Lenny thanking me for the gifts, saying he appreciated everything and again, reassuring me that we would talk *soon*. I proceeded to the birthday bash and had an overdue blast drinking, dancing, flirting and just catching up with my girl. Nevertheless, when the bottles stopped popping and the music stopped banging, my reality remained the same.

On my way home, I planned out how my next encounter with him would go. He wanted to talk and while I wanted to listen, I also needed to make sure letting go was not optional. The next night I anticipated our meet. I was nervous that he'd cancel on me but at the same time mentally prepared.

I headed to his crib after I got off work. When I arrived, his truck wasn't there. I called him and he didn't answer. *Maybe he had to make a quick run,* I thought. I sat there listening to music in my truck. After about fifteen minutes, a text from him came through:

Lenny: I'm so sorry. Something came up that I must take care of.

Me: Its cool. I'm here parked. I'll just wait until you get back. No worries ☺

Lenny: Lets plan for tomorrow. I won't be back until like 3a.m.

Me: Ugh…okay. Just give me a heads up if plans change.

Lenny blew me off the next night assuring we'd talk the next night. That following night when I called to confirm, he responded via his predictable mode of text:

"Look, I really do care about you and it's not you, it's me. I can't be in a relationship right now because I first must get myself together. I'm really sorry and I hope that we can still be friends," he texted me.

My heart dropped as I felt this coming but denied it. I called him after that to let him know I could handle us just being "friends", but my calls went unanswered. My texts went unanswered. I became a ghost to him.

I was in disbelief. *How could this be happening? How could something so nurtured and satisfying have turned into something so unrewarding?* The days painfully turned into weeks and it was so easy for him to forget about me. He blocked my number from receiving calls and texts, and even blocked me on Facebook. I downloaded various connection apps to reach him in alternative ways, but he'd never respond. At one point, I convinced myself that I didn't care by blocking his number, only to unblock it days, sometimes only hours later, since missing his imaginary call hurt way worse than him not calling.

I would still see Lenny here and there, but it was almost as if he were intentionally dodging me. He would walk past me as if I was non-existent, never daring enough to make eye contact. I changed my hair, jogged three miles a day three times a week, arrived early and stayed late at work in hopes of seeing him … in hopes of being *seen*.

He ignored me day after day and my efforts went unnoticed. My anger became dangerous. My desire for revenge became toxic. My bottle of Moscato and my pen were my two best friends.

Last Time

How could you walk away without saying a word?
You treated me in a way that I didn't deserve.
Ignoring my texts and blocking my calls.
Transparently reflecting how I meant nothing at all.
You had me waiting and waiting for you.

But to my heart you just couldn't be true.
Perhaps I wanted more than you were willing to give.
Had me contemplating was it even worth it to live.
You made a fool of me when I rocked with you tough.
Never once did you put up a fight when you felt shit get rough.
You're supposed to be a "lion" but you chose to run and hide.
Playing in these streets and holding on to your pride.
You wear it on your shoulder like it's a fucking gold trophy.
Probably somewhere getting drunk or popping a rollie.
I hope karma comes and takes a bite out of your ass.
I hope she breaks your fucking heart and have an abortion at the last....
Minute...because the last time you were deep up in it,
You played Trey Songz "Last Time."
But I couldn't read in between the lines.
I thought that it was just your shit.
But I didn't comprehend too quick.
Must have been hypnotized by the dick.
So I let you dip your candlestick.
And when the flame was no longer lit.
You kissed me for what you knew.
and what I had no clue was our very last time.

I hated to do anything or be around anyone. Positivity was my worst enemy and TJ saw firsthand when my world came crashing down. I treated TJ badly when I was with Lenny and I knew that it was just the cycle of karma returning its favor. No one is exempt. No matter how long you were loyal and got screwed over time and time again, the moment you change roles and go from being the *screw-ee* to the *screw-er,* you automatically earn your notch on the never-ending chain of karma, and you never know when it will knock on your door.

TJ felt my distance and sorrow, and while I caused my own share of grief to him, he still allowed himself to become subjective to my emotions, showing sensitivity.

He didn't pressure me for answers. He knows me well enough to know that I will come out of my shell when I'm comfortable and ready to face to world. I was prepared to face my choices alone, but TJ made me feel that even though I pushed him away, we're still in this together.

I wasn't sure if he felt that he owed me something or if he genuinely wanted to make our marriage work, but either way, I appreciated the moral support. He and I knew that it would take a whole lot of doing and a lot less saying from the both of us in order to make *us* a considerable option. So many things had changed between us over these last few months and while I own up to my wrongdoing, it doesn't change the fact that those events transpired. Our priorities became more and more out of sync with each passing day. Religion was no longer a priority for us and I couldn't help but wonder if my lack of faith was the reason behind my pain and suffering.

Although in my heart I knew that the affair with Leonard was over, I knew that it wasn't by choice. I still held on to the possibility of what could be. As a result, I was never able to fully give myself to my husband. It wasn't that I didn't think TJ was worth a shot as he does have the potential to be a great mate, and our sex life has been blazing when we're mentally connected. I just didn't want to get *us* back to a happy place and then Lenny decides to come back. I'd end up hurting TJ again. The power I gave Lenny was sickening.

TJ and I decided to do something we didn't do in the beginning. We decided to start over simply as only friends, getting to know one another all over again.

I wanted to go back because it was comforting to my soul, but on the same token I knew that things would still be the same because we were still the same. I wasn't willing to be the change that I wished to see, and I wanted more than what I was willing to give. I was hurt by the two men who I loved the most and the reality of it all toughened my skin and made me resilient to bullshit.

I longed to have a strong financial partnership with TJ. He was so accustomed to spending his money as he pleased. There was no "us". It was the money *I* made, which went to bills and everything under the sun, and then the money he made, which went to whatever bad habits and guilty pleasures he indulged in. I rarely questioned his spending habits and he took full advantage of that.

TJ was raised by all women and he had a rough childhood to say the least. While I love his family dearly and empathize with their circumstances, he never had a good example of a positive man in his life. Unfortunately it has been shown time and time again.

However, it's hard to do better when you don't know what better looks like. A part of me feels that I contributed to enabling him since I never required him to behave differently. I needed a partner, not a crutch, but I never demanded him to have any responsibility in our finances. I was content with how little as well as how much he did. I guess it's true when they say, "Why buy the cow if you can get the milk for free?"

I took great pride in my independence before TJ. I never wanted to just sit around and be taken care of by a man. I've always been business-minded, continuously strategizing to find ways to build our personal brands, but it takes willingness and the ability to compromise.

I have a vision and in a strong partnership there must be vision as he who lacks vision lacks purpose. I spent so much time on that aspect of business that I forgot to do what makes *me* happy.

I wanted to finish my degree, I wanted to write endlessly, and I also wanted to go back to making my massage oil candles and selling them online and locally. My business was my baby until I lost all my candle making supplies and formulas to a natural disaster.

My husband and I rented a storage unit to store the business supplies for the two small businesses. One day in early summer of 2016, a terrible storm unexpectedly swept through the mid-south with winds so strong that the metal door and roofing was ripped right off our storage unit, along with six other units. The units flooded from the heavy rains and the wind caused severe damage. The area was taped off and condemned for nearly two months and with sweltering triple-digit temps, I knew without a doubt that my two hundred pounds of soy wax had melted, not to mention all of my essential oils had been exposed to direct sunlight.

When we were finally allowed to take inventory of our belongings, which were basically outdoor in the open, we weren't surprised to learn that everything was destroyed. From dirt and debris to insects and rodent poop—nothing was salvageable. We had only been in the unit for a couple months prior to the flood and we opted for their minimal coverage as we didn't think for once a disaster of that nature would occur. We replaced what we could in order of priority and my candle making supplies did not make the list as it didn't nearly have the potential to generate revenue like his commercial cleaning company.

I was tired of putting my dreams on hold and making investments with zero returns. How could I expect the world to believe in me when I didn't have the courage to believe in myself? I felt broken, but I still had a vision and it was my vision that kept my hope alive. I knew that I wanted better and deserved better, but I just didn't know where to start to better myself or my situation. I tried to turn back to religion, but my soul was still just too invidious. I knew that it was never my place to question my fate and I just didn't feel worthy of forgiveness, so I never asked for it.

The closeness between the two of us felt real, but I knew that there was still so much hurt between TJ and me. He started to come around more often. Staying over every few days turned into a couple weeks at a time. I agreed to give answers in due time, but as time passed, his patience became weary. I knew where the anger was coming from, and as a result, neither one of us were truly satisfying the other. We knew that even as friends, it would take time to build courage and trust.

The friendship bond that TJ and I were rebuilding was evolving more and more with each passing day. It felt good to fall in love with my husband all over again. It felt good to make love and not feel guilty or slutty about it afterwards. However, it felt bad to pretend like my feelings for Lenny went away overnight, but I couldn't bear to hurt TJ again. I knew that I had to move on from this inexorable obsession for answers, but I just didn't know how. TJ always told me to practice what I preached, so I vowed to be truthful about everything, and I did...

Chapter 6

THE TRUTH

O NE RANDOM NIGHT after an unusually long day at work, TJ came over and the two of us shared a bottle of wine. I decided to make that the night I own my truths. I can remember taking the last of the Pink Moscato in the bottle to the head and inhaling deeply. *Here it goes,* I thought to myself before I proceeded to reveal my most sacred truths to this man that I knew loved me. Last time I was reassured that the truth wouldn't change anything, it changed everything. *Was this a risk worth taking? Was the whole truth really necessary? Would knowing this really help the situation?* While I wasn't sure the answers to any of the questions that I pondered, one thing I knew for certain was that the deception was weighing heavily on my heart and I needed to do this for me as much as he needed me to do it for him.

I started off with Matthew. I met Matthew about a month after the affair with Lenny ended, while TJ and I were living in separate homes. I was on my way to work and stopped at my favorite Shell gas station for my usual 8.4oz can of Red Bull and single Black & Mild cigar. On my way inside, I couldn't help but notice this fine ass, caramel skin-toned, 6'5" sexy brotha in a white Nissan Armada. I caught his eye when I walked out the store and I knew that I had his full attention, as I made sure he knew I was feeling him too. I'm not really sure where my magic set of big balls came from, but on my way out I pulled up beside his SUV and rolled my window down. He did the same.

"What's your name?"

"Matthew."

"So Matthew, are we just going to keep smiling and go on with our day or are we going to exchange numbers and get to know one another a little better?" I said to him smiling.

I tore the bottom piece of my receipt off and wrote my name and number down on it and passed it to him as he was close enough to accept it effortlessly. He said that he would text me right away and to lock him in as he too was on his way to work. I heard the alert sound through my vehicle's Bluetooth. I was running late for work and I told him that I looked forward to talking with him soon.

I pulled off like a race car trying to make up for lost time. When I finally got to a red light I decided to lock his number in before I forget and delete it as I hate a cluttered inbox with unknown or miscellaneous numbers. When I checked my text messages I learned that it wasn't a message from Matthew earlier, but an auto alert for the purchase I had just made with my Visa.

"Ugh" … my stomach dropped. To make matters worse, it dawned on me that I gave him the wrong digits. My dyslexia got the best of me as I reversed the last two digits that I wrote down for him. I felt like such a klutz as my caramel mocha latte fantasy ended before it even began, and for a girl who doesn't drink coffee, I was willing to have a taste.

When I got to work my two good friends, Aaliyah and Trisha, immediately picked up on my tension. I was still in denial about Lenny, telling everyone that we were still good, but the ones who really *knew* me, knew that it was all a lie. I was closer to Aaliyah spiritually, in awe of her wisdom and knowledge. Trisha and I too have a special connection as I appreciate her poise and overall finesse.

I acted as if I wasn't fazed and didn't notice that Lenny and I were drifting apart, but it was real and it affected me in its every aspect. I was only left to assume and there is nothing worse than making assumptions. I wanted answers and the unknown drove me insane. I didn't want to think about religion, relationships, hang out with my girlfriends or even entertain men from my past. The world as I knew was filled with deception and lies. I almost thought for a brief moment that I could beat the odds and win without going to war.

"What's wrong with you?" asked Aaliyah.

I continued working on my project as if I didn't hear her talking to me. She walked up to me and knocked my mid-sized stack of chronologically organized documents to the floor. There was an awkward silence as we had a stare-off. She adjusted her eyeglasses with her index finger and we continued to assume the thoughts of the other. Trisha laughed to break the ice. I chuckled slightly, shaking my head as I kneeled to pick up the documents.

"What's wrong? For real." Aaliyah asked as she helped me pick up the papers.

"Is it that obvious?" I asked her.

"Now you know I can pick up on your vibes and while you don't have to tell me what it is, just know that I'm here for you if you need me," she said as she smiled warmly. She gave me a hug and tears filled my eyes.

Aaliyah pulled me to the break room and while I was too embarrassed to tell her how Lenny played the shit out of me, I gave her the latest update between me and TJ and told her that it was all just taking its toll. I ended it by venting to her about Matthew and the wrong number ordeal. She listened as she always does and ultimately reassured me that everything will work itself out according to God's plan. While I knew that she was right, the reality of it still pained me deeply. After the whole Lenny situation, I was really confused between the things that I desired and the things that were destined. It caused me to question things I dared to never and to keep me somewhat sane, I just shut it out completely.

The next day I had to go to work an hour earlier for a meeting. I drank myself to sleep the night before and woke up just in the nick of time for work. I hurried by the gas station for my usual Red Bull and cigar, and to my surprise Matthew pulled up beside me in his white SUV. We both joked about the coincidence being a little ironic but were equally grateful for it.

I apologized about the phone number mix up but felt foolish as he told me that he never got around to texting me yesterday. I anticipated his call that night, but he never called. The next day I didn't run into him and after another day passed by, I was already over that situation.

The following day I was awakened to breakfast-in-bed along with a single stem red rose. Afterwards TJ went about his work day and I went jogging at the park to relieve some stress. When I got home, I couldn't wait to get out of my sweaty clothes and get a short nap in before work. I set an alarm to wake up in an hour to shower, but in the meantime I changed into a pink dry-fit tank, some pink "cheeky" shorts, and put on a pair of knee length black socks. I jammed my "Mint Condition" Pandora station and felt instant relief when I laid on my pillow-top mattress.

Have you ever wanted to go to sleep so desperately but the thoughts inside your head, you know, the voice that only you hear when you read these words in silence ... have they ever been so loud to whereas you couldn't fall asleep? Well, call me crazy but that was what I was experiencing, and it was driving me insane. My brain was going non-stop and the only thing I wanted to do was rest as I had a full day ahead. An incoming call from an unknown number came through. I was hesitant to answer and wished I wouldn't have ... it was Matthew.

He told me some crazy story about how he dropped his phone in a puddle of water and the phone-in-dry rice trick didn't work. He talked about how he just moved back to Memphis and started his new truck driving job. He claimed he didn't want to pay a phone bill for a phone that doesn't work, so his phone is now off and this is his "partner's number". He urged me to not call it back. Blah, blah, blah … all the red flags were there, but I still proceeded to give him the benefit of the doubt and entertain his foolishness.

We talked for a few minutes more and he quickly picked up on my restlessness. I couldn't deny that my bullshit radar was sounding off as reflected in my incredulous tone of voice. Matthew insisted that it was imperative we talk in person, adding that he wouldn't mind coming over to give me a hug as he *missed* seeing me. I was very reluctant as he was in every aspect a stranger. Moreover, I told him that 'I don't do house visits', especially being I didn't even know him. He pleaded that he wasn't a psychotic serial killer and he'd be the one taking the greater risk as I could be armed and dangerous or could plan to set him up. While there was some truth in his statement, I knew that I was playing a dangerous game if I opened Pandora's box.

I could hear Matthew's loud beats as soon as he pulled into my driveway. I put on my black open front cardigan and went outside. I greeted him with a warm smile at my gate. I motioned for him to come towards me with one hand in the air, as I tugged on the back of my shorts with the other hand to cover my cheeks. *Am I really doing this?* I thought aloud as I looked at him brushing his waves after he closed his door.

"Damn, you look different," he said as he squeezed my body tightly.

He was strong. I could feel my feet lift off the ground and my ass jiggle when returned to the surface. I don't have a big booty by any means and in most clothes I find my butt to be unflattering, but it's the kind of butt that you don't realize is there until the clothes come off or are barely on, and in this case they were barely on. I was leaving nothing to this man's imagination. I knew that super-slut was the image I was portraying, and I knew that by doing this I would be ruining any chance of anything serious with this man, but I didn't care. I hated men with a vengeance and only wanted revenge, one heartbreak at a time.

"Man, you've got some nosy neighbors," he said making mention to the older lady who lives next door and somehow manages to know the 411 on everything and everybody. Day, night, sunny, stormy, this lady never misses a beat and keeps the "tea" freshly brewed. Since TJ has moved out, he makes it a priority to have full, extensive conversations with her whenever he stops by the house. She thinks that I'm "stuck up", but I've always been slow to trust. She's never taken the time to get to know me, and vice versa, so she and I don't have a real neighborly relationship.

I could only imagine the story she was creating in her mind.

He and I stood outside and talked for about five minutes. I told him that I had to get ready for work.

"I hope I didn't waste your time," I said to him as I walked back towards the house. I still had over two hours before I had to go in to work and my bed was calling my name as I could finally feel my thoughts slowing down.

"Hey!" he called out to me right before I closed the door. I turned around and stuck my head out of the storm door.

"What?"

"Do you mind if I use your bathroom?"

"No! I thought you lived less than ten minutes from here?"

"I do, but I'm heading in the opposite direction. You can stand outside the bathroom door if you don't trust me."

"Ugh...fine. Make it quick sir."

I'd be lying if I said I was comfortable allowing him inside my home, my comfort zone, my personal space, but I knew that the damage was already done the moment I gave him my address. Prior to moving here, I had my home robbed in the past twice, so this was all way too foolish.

I pulled up the doors to the bedrooms as I walked ahead of him. I guided him to the bathroom and waited in the adjacent hallway. "Breakin' My Heart" blasted from my bedroom and I sang its every lyric as the music drowned out my naturally drunken karaoke voice. I could hear the water in the sink running, which meant he was finishing up and if it took longer than another thirty seconds then that meant he was snooping through my shit.

He came out of the bathroom smiling and bobbing his head to the beat while he lip-synched the lyrics.

"What do you know about this with your lil' young self?" I asked returning the smile. I assumed he was at the least younger than me.

I was disappointed to learn that he was five years younger than me, as if I hadn't learned my lesson of being guided by fools. It's difficult to take someone down a road you haven't traveled or stepped foot upon.

"I love music. I love to dance. I just moved back here from the A-T-L. I teach choreography too," Matthew said to me as he spun around like Chris Brown.

"Of course", I responded sarcastically.

I was already getting sick from the self-centeredness. There surely had to be a medical term for this. I could sense that he was the type of guy not used to hearing the word "no".

"I see you have kids," he said slowly as he strangely stared at the framed collage of my children displayed on the tangerine colored center wall. I could see him trying to figure out how many kids I actually had as the collage features random, fun pictures of them from the age of two to the teenage years. I didn't bother to clarify either as you could clearly see it was the same kids in all the pictures, just growing as kids seemingly do.

"Yep! My babies are the best part of me and I wouldn't trade them for the world," I said defensively.

He told me about his "little one" and admitted that while he wasn't in a relationship with his son's mother, they platonically reside under one roof. Now if only I were naïve enough to believe such circumstances existed. We were making it closer and closer to the front door. I could see his steps were becoming slower and slower.

"Can I get another hug?" he asked.

I almost felt sorry as the attempt was beyond pathetic. When I hugged him, I felt no magic or chemistry. Matthew embraced me as if there were sparks igniting between us.

"You smell so good. I can only imagine how good you taste," he said in a whispering tone into my ear.

I'm not sure if it was a tickle or a quiver, but I could feel the chills travel down my spine.

"Is that so?" I asked in an inquisitive manner.

All I could think about was Lenny and I just wanted to make it go away.

"What are you doing tonight?" I asked him.

"No plans as of now. Would love for it to be you, but I understand if that can't be," he said to me. My laughter was impishly misleading.

"Is it okay if I break down this cigar before I leave? I just need to use your trash can," he asked.

We sat down on my leather loveseat. I watched him break down the cigar, then his small portion of weed on my coffee table. We made small talk and the more I listened, the more I realized we had absolutely nothing in common beyond a mere physical attraction.

When he finished, he placed his rolled blunt behind his ear, cleaned up his mess and scooted closer towards me on the loveseat.

"I don't have any plans I can think of, so I *should* be able to see you tonight," I said hesitantly as I stood up.

He reached for my arm and pulled me towards him.

"Dance with me," he begged as "What Kind of Man Would I Be" echoed from my speaker.

"No!" I said in an annoyed tone as this man was out of his rabbit mind.

I was terribly frustrated and sat back down. He stood up and just when I thought he was about to leave, he started to dance on me. Well, it was more of a risqué strip tease. I was in complete shock at his audacity. I mean talk about new age confidence!

He grinded and maneuvered his body flawlessly on mine. My sultry glances said that I enjoyed what he was doing, and he wasn't ashamed to test the limits. He kneeled between my legs and rested his hands on my thighs.

"I know that this is soon but I'm really feeling you," he said right before he politely asked if he could kiss my lips. I nodded my head yes as I seductively bit my bottom lip. The sweet taste of cocoa lingered on my lips from my moisturizing flavored lip balm.

I prepared to embrace the taste of his lips. I closed my eyes as I felt his body move in towards mine.

My eyes opened slowly as his tongue circled around the butterfly tattoos on my upper thigh. I was frozen and insecure as my body was still sweaty from my workout. I wanted to yell "stop", but it felt amazingly refreshing. He placed my long legs over his shoulders and before I knew it, his face was immersed in my ocean of love as he slid my shorts to the side and gripped my thighs. I moaned so loudly I feared the nosy neighbor would hear. After all, TJ had been in and out a lot lately.

"Let's go to the back," I said to him as I was beyond paranoid.

He came up for air and said, "Okay, hold on tight."

"Whoa! Hold on, what are you—"

Before I could finish my sentence, he lifted me up high as if I weighed nothing. My thick legs were dangling over his shoulders and back, and he clinched my ass in his hands. My body tensed up and my thighs squeezed his face tightly as I was scared I'd fall, considering his view was obstructed.

He allowed my voice to guide him to the bedroom. The dirty plates from breakfast-in-bed before my morning jog were still on the night-stand. I couldn't pretend that this wasn't wrong. I didn't know what to do and I reacted by doing nothing.

When he arrived to the bedroom, I had to lower my head downwards so I wouldn't hit the doorframe. He gently placed me on the bed and picked up where he left off, conquering the skill of oral pleasure.

"You taste so good," he said as he devoured me like it was his last supper.

Despite the ecstatic feeling, I was in way over my head and in total disbelief. I couldn't believe that this man was so willing to literally dive in head first without a life jacket. He drank my waters until my rivers overflowed, savoring its every delight. When he stood up he pulled his shirt over his head. I admired his gym physique as he was very easy on the eye. My trance was broken when I saw him removing his belt buckle.

"Whoa! Slow down man," I said as I jumped up.

He kissed my lips and told me how badly he wanted to *feel* me.

"Do you at least have a condom playboy?" I asked as I tried to catch my breath in between his aggressive kisses that smothered my entire face.

"I'm safe baby. I just want to put it in and take it right out. I promise," Matthew said to me.

"This isn't a good idea. Maybe you could come back tonight … better prepared. Look, I really have to go to work and I think you should go," I said as I definitely pulled away from him. I took a few steps back, holding my cardigan for dear life.

"Fuck tonight, I want this right now!"

Matthew caught me off guard and shoved me in my back. I lost my balance from the shock and stumbled onto the bed. He forcefully grabbed the back of my neck, holding it down with one hand. I could feel the pressure from my crossed wrists firmly pressing into my back as his body leaned against me.

He pushed my face into the mattress as he forced himself inside of me. I tried to lift my body off the bed to gasp for air. I could hardly breathe. He was too strong, and furthermore I knew that I led him on.

Sexually, my body responded to his as if it were partaking in a blissful sexual encounter. I still can recall just feeling numb. After about maybe two minutes of zoning out and hoping *it* would end, I just remember him saying, "Oh, shit I'm about to cum!"

"No the hell you aren't!" I said as I was finally able to push him off me due to his weakened sexual state before climax.

He looked at me dumb-founded, as though nothing was wrong.

"I was *just* getting ready to cum," he said in a frustrated tone as he pulled up his boxer briefs.

He stormed out of my bedroom and I immediately locked the door. I traded my shorts in for a pair of sweatpants and a plush robe. I cut my music off completely, so I could listen to his footsteps as they made their exit along my hard wood floors. I was startled by my one-hour alarm, immediately rushing over to silence it. I peeked through my blackout curtains since I didn't have the courage to leave my room until I saw his truck backing out of my driveway. I looked across the walkway and I could see my neighbor peeping out of her blinds.

When I knew that Matthew was gone for good, I immediately secured my home. As I turned the lock, I could feel the tears trickle down my cheek. I was so confused. I felt so empty and so worthless. I was trying to mentally make sense of what just happened; trying to pretend that nothing even happened at all. *Had I become that promiscuously desperate?*

I ran a hot shower and held my knees to my chest as my tears became one with the flowing waters. Hot as a sauna, the bathroom quickly filled with steam. My wrists were slightly bruised and my body was tender to the touch. I wasn't quite sure if it was from the temperature of the water or the physical aggression, but because of the blame I placed on myself, I chose to further endure the pain. All I could see was a blur and all that I felt was hollowness. I wanted everything to end … I just wanted all the pain from all the wounds to just go away by any means necessary.

Later that night when I got off work and made it home, Matthew pulled into my driveway less than five minutes after I arrived home— uninvited. I had no clue that he was coming over as we didn't confirm anything and I sure as hell wasn't about to answer the door after that

lier. He knocked steadily and heavily. My cell phone began

ff and I hurried to mute it.

ming call from a *Private* number showed up on my caller id screen. I ignored the call. The "anonymous" caller continued to call my cell phone back to back. The knocking eventually stopped. I lit the candle centered on my marble dining room table and sat on my living room floor in darkness, listening to the silence of the night. I never heard the vehicle back out of the driveway and I was too afraid to go to the window and look out.

I heard a loud knock on my bedroom window. I could hear the window shaking from the vibrations of the force. I knew it was Matthew, but you couldn't have dared me to look. I felt ashamed and defamed. I grabbed my cell phone and proceeded to call the police. While on hold for an operator, I finally heard the sound I was waiting to hear ... Matthew's truck backing out of the driveway. I hung up the phone quickly as I assumed that they would say that the whole scenario was my fault, and I know oh too well how it feels to be made to feel that the message wasn't clear.

After ensuring that the coast was clear and my perimeters were safe, I decided to clear my head and go for a drive. I talked to Troy, my absolute best male friend, my entire drive until I made it back inside my home safely. No matter how many "girlfriends" I have and adore, it takes a man to understand the mindset of a man and vice versa. In my opinion, every woman needs that one male friend who's truly an adviser. Someone there to listen in time of need as well as give authentic, unbiased advice. More importantly, someone who has no sexual expectations from you. It's one of my most innocent and cherished friendships and most of all, I've never had to question its authenticity. It saddens me at how I'm more close to someone I've only known for a couple years than people I've known my whole life.

As I continued to reveal the details of my affair and the proceeding pain to TJ, the more I felt relieved, almost as if a weight was being lifted off my shoulders. However, the more in depth I went into the affair,

the more I could sense an emotional drift. He sat ther
and just listened. Despite us being separated at the ti
change the fact that I was legally his wife and committin
could only imagine how hard it would be to take in the t   ͜ͅ ᴜ₁at l
shared with him, but I'm giving him an option to choose. My truth
is my truth and I will be fair and not make the decision for him, as
it was done to me.

I know that it may sound crazy, but all I ever wanted to do was "know", and then with knowing the truth, make a conscious and sound decision. The truth alone is never painful, only our reactions to the truth. We can choose to be consumed by the things that we can't control, such as the actions of others, or we can choose to make the best out of every situation and not take offense to the things done and said by others. Honesty and transparency are now a rarity, but they're essential in living in peace. I can only dream of coexisting in a world where people aren't afraid of the truth; where all people gracefully receive and respect the truth.

I recently found myself socializing with an Asian psychologist for a lengthy period. As an unmarried man who grew up in the Philippines, he was so disgusted with the American culture and its lack of cultural values. His philosophy is that the American culture measures wealth materialistically, such as with the purchasing of expensive homes and owning multiple luxury vehicles. On the other hand, he said that *his* culture measures wealth in the form of a man's quality of work-life balance. He broke it down further to say that it entails being able to provide your family with life's essentials and physically using the time away from work, and the things of the world, to bond and develop an unbreakable closeness, establishing a foundation of loyalty and humility.

While the doctor and I discussed topics from the harmfulness of social media and its widespread popularity, to the gap in cultural literacy, to the belief and testimonial experiences of karma and its boomerang effect, what weighed in the heaviest was the overall difference in the value of life. We put so much stress on ourselves to be perfect for society, perfect for our children, friends, colleagues and even spouses, when at the end of each and every day, we are all human beings coexisting in the same universe. Whether or not we choose to admit it, we all have our own struggles and insecurities, as that's what make us perfectly imperfect.

Chapter 7

THE INSANITY

ALTHOUGH I WAS once again reassured that my truth would bear no consequences, I felt that my husband was disappointed in me and his actions proved me right. He didn't know who I was anymore and oftentimes I questioned my own personal identity. While he was and has always been there for me, it was different this time. His "hi's" and "bye's" were dry and he even stopped asking me for sex. He went out of his way to not need me.

I could tell that his guards were up high with me and his trust was out of the window, but what's craziest is that he already knew the truth before I told him, so why did knowing the insignificant details hurt so much? Maybe this is why he chose to not tell me … maybe he always knew how much the truth would hurt me, so he chose to lie to protect a fragile heart that shouldn't have been broken.

While TJ adjusted to his new perception of me, I adapted to his emotional changes. I accepted that the chivalry was obsolete and only our true desire to reconnect and be restored would bring it back. I felt that I wasn't mentally ready to be a wife as I lost myself in the absence of loyalty. I gave up on love a long time ago, although I've always been in love with the *thought* of being in love. I allowed myself to be so blinded by its conceptual beauty that I ignored and bypassed the most compromising of things. I was afraid of the past but feared the future even more. I just wanted TJ to genuinely be my friend for once. I was so fed up with titles. I just wanted to be left alone and stripped of all my defining titles, except for being a mother.

My mother moved in with us for a very short period of time while she waited on her new place of residence to become readily available. She knew something was going on between TJ and I, but she never asked questions nor allowed me to voice my opinion about our marital dilemmas. It was almost as if she wasn't there, both physically and emotionally. She stayed in the girl's room almost up until it was time for her to prepare for work each day. Also, with the kids only home on weekends, none of us ever cooked real meals, and when we did, it was usually small, personal-sized portions or just enough for a one-time serving. My mom would have her daily mid-morning coffee since she sleeps in late, but other than that, we would rarely interact.

My mom and I arrive home around the same time every night. Although I get off work thirty minutes prior to her scheduled shift end, I travel a fair distance whereas her job is in the neighborhood. Regardless to who arrives home first, she always parks on the left side of the carport whereas he and I park in the primary spot. TJ is almost always flying in the driveway like a bat out of hell right behind the two of us each night. Most nights I sit and wait in my truck until he arrives to ensure the safety of the perimeters before I exit my vehicle. I usually don't care where he parks as he's always on-the-go, but my only request is to not be blocked in Thursday and Friday nights. I typically work so early those subsequent mornings that it's a dread to have to wake up someone so early, then wait on them to move their vehicle from behind mine.

Friday, October 13th arrived and began with unexpected setbacks. I had to be at work at 6:30a.m.. I had my alarm clock routinely set for 5:30a.m., giving me twenty minutes to get ready and thirty-five minutes to make it to work in early morning traffic. I showered the night before and prepared my work clothes as my little time savers, so I would just have to focus on the small stuff like freshening up and grabbing a muffin or yogurt.

I awoke that morning on time and even had a lunch in hand on my way out of the door. As I hurried outside, I was shocked to find that I was blocked in the driveway. I was frustrated as it was early, but before I could storm back inside with a vengeance, TJ was walking out the door pulling his sweatshirt over his head while he yawned. I felt a moment of instant relief as I got inside my vehicle. *What is he doing?* I wondered as he slammed the door to his truck and ran back inside the house. The clock read 6:05a.m. but I knew I could still make it on time with minimal rushing.

When he came back outside, he secured the house and proceeded to his truck. While I got lost in time wondering where he could be going this early in the morning after only being home for a few hours, I didn't realize that I was still sitting in the driveway five minutes after he locked the house. I looked into my rearview mirror and I saw him pacing back and forth outside. I stepped outside my truck, shivering from the early morning temps. I asked him what was wrong.

TJ informed me that he locked his keys inside his vehicle with the engine running.

"You've got to be kidding me. This cannot be happening to me today!" I said in rage.

I could feel the panic and anxiety taking over as I watched him attempt to pry his door open using various objects and tools. Time seemed to pass at a rapid rate as I found myself calling my supervisor to inform her that I'd be late, but would definitely be there to open the office before its scheduled time.

"What are you doing?" TJ yelled out as I got out of my truck and proceeded to the house. My face was cold from the wind chill and tears fell as I turned towards him.

"I'm about to wake my mom up and see if I can use her car and somehow bring it back to her on my break," I said to him.

"What are you crying for? You're always giving up on me. You offered to help me not one single time and still I said I got you. If you want to wake her up then go ahead, that's on you, but I almost have it unlocked," he said as you could hear the strain in his voice as he nearly lifted the latch.

I laughed as I looked at the time. The clock read 6:43a.m.

"What's so funny?" he asked in an arrogant tone as he finally lifted the latch and unlocked his vehicle.

There was no way my driving skills could pull off a twenty-five-minute commute in roughly fifteen minutes. I needed him to speed like a lightning bolt and get me to work as he's done in the past so many times before.

I cut off my truck and walked over to his vehicle.

"I'm not about to take you to work then have to deal with getting your ass when you get off. No!" he said to me.

My eyes and ears couldn't believe what I was hearing. I was in total disbelief.

"I didn't ask for you to block me in the driveway!" I yelled to him.

He reiterated that he was not taking me to work and began to back out of the driveway.

My heart was racing and I didn't know what to do. I felt like I was losing everything. My lover abandoned me, my kids don't live with me and now I'm about to lose my job. I got back inside my truck and pulled out the driveway, heading in the opposite direction of my job. My phone rang immediately and it was TJ. I declined the calls each time they came in. The vehicle in front of me made an abrupt stop to avoid from hitting a stalled vehicle ahead.

I wasn't surprised to see TJ selfishly halting traffic, causing a lane block on the narrow street with one lane of traffic in each direction. I couldn't go forward without ramming him, to the right was a ditch, and the line of traffic behind me was longer than Third Street as all the other cars were going around us. I put my blinkers on and just sat there … thinking.

"Where the hell are you going?" he yelled through the windows I refused to roll down.

I focused my view on the side mirrors as I rolled down the window slightly and muted my music so he could hear me clearly.

"I don't care about anything *anymore*. I'm about to drive my car off the road or crash it into something, so please just leave me alone and quit ruining everybody's day on account of ours!" I said to him.

The opposite lane finally cleared and I quickly made my move, maneuvering around his vehicle, only this time I was heading in the direction of home to throw him off. It was one minute to opening and there were zero chances of making it on time. My cell phone rang steadily from TJ and my inbox and voicemail was flooded with messages from my supervisor. I began to have a panic attack. I turned my phone off completely and just drove. I didn't know what to do to make the reality of it all not be true. I didn't care about the hurt or the consequences, I just wanted the pain to stop.

As bizarre as it may seem, the next thing I remember was waking up in the emergency room partially clothed with IV's hooked up to my arm and people asking me suicide-related questions. I didn't recall driving there nor being transported there. My purse was on the faded green leather chair next to me. I could see my truck keys dangling out of its back pocket. My eyes were sore and I was still confused and overwhelmed by the whole situation. I powered my phone back on to find a series of missed calls, text messages and voicemails.

While there were many questions unanswered, one thing for certain is that it was well past 10a.m and the truth remained the same. I felt the anxiety building up rapidly again. I yelled for a nurse and immediately asked for a bag, bucket or anything within reach. In the nick of time, I filled two bags with vomit on an empty stomach which stunned me since I was down to eating only one meal a day. I was terrified of my physical appearance being the reason I wasn't desirable for men.

Needless to say, there was some relief after releasing that, but the tears were in my eyes and the hurt still remained in my heart. I wiped my face with the generic box of facial tissue on the bedside tray. In the hallway I could hear commotion of some sort.

"You let me hear my wife tell me that she doesn't want me here!" I heard a familiar voice aggressively telling security through the thin curtain that separated me from them.

My young and beautiful nurse Alexis stepped back inside the room and informed me that it was totally up to my discretion and I did not have to have "visitors" if I wasn't ready. That confused me more as if she was under the assumption we were having differences, unless I told her something and clearly didn't remember.

I told her that it was okay to let TJ in. She stared him up and down as she opened the curtain for him to enter, then rolled her eyes as he walked past her. To give us privacy, she stepped outside the small room and drew the curtain behind her. There was apparent tension between the two of them, however I was too mentally exhausted to pick my brain on the many possibilities of why. He walked over to the bed where I sat in an upright position. He leaned in to hug me and I embraced him back. His initial reaction was worry, then it immediately went to anger, blame and insult.

The nurse came in and out my room more times within five minutes than she did my entire time thus far, at least that I can recall. While I found it to be quite amusing, her presence angered him even more. Alexis, however, was not shy about asking him if he had a problem with her. I diffused the situation between the two of them and reassured her that it was just a misunderstanding and to continue to do her job. She took my vitals and noted an increase in my blood pressure. She asked TJ to step outside of the room. I motioned for him to go ahead, assuring him that he was coming right back in when she finished up.

Alexis started off by saying that this was off the records as it's not coming from *nurse* Alexis but *friend* Alexis. She said that while she didn't know the details of what it was I was going through, she knew that I was very distressed and had been hurt by something or someone. I tried to hold back my tears, but they had a power of their own and trickled down shamefully. She continued to say that one thing for certain was that I was beautiful, intelligent and I deserved the very best that life had to offer and to never settle for anything less than that. I laughed and told her thank you, but I was a complete mess. I could feel the puffiness in my face from the constant crying. She chuckled slightly then cleared her throat.

I felt a chill as the mood shifted from softhearted to stern. She proceeded to inform me that this was *on the records* now and my physician has recommended me to go to a behavioral healthcare facility. I couldn't wrap my brain around anything that she was saying. All I could comprehend was "go to."

I see places like that on television all the time and I was damned if that was my destiny. My tears continuously flowed as I pleaded for it to all just be over with.

"What do you want to be over and done with?" Alexis asked me puzzled.

"Everything ... all of *this*," I cried to her, never looking up again. I could hear the torturing sound of her pen going across the clipboard rapidly.

"Can you please get my husband for me?" I asked her.

"Sure thing," she said as she rubbed the center of my back gently.

My husband came back inside and sat at the edge of the bed. His eyes were filled with tears as it hurt him to know that we were right back to square one. I loved him undeniably, but just wasn't certain that the good outweighed the bad. We sat there in silence as there was really nothing left to say.

He looked me in my eyes and while no words were spoken, I heard everything that was being said. He laid his head across my lap and I massaged his temple.

"Now what?" he asked as if he was dreading the answer.

I didn't know what to say because I didn't even know the right thing to do anymore. I sighed heavily.

"Maybe they're right, maybe this *is* what I need…"

Chapter 8

THE FEAR

THE DAY CAME and went and was not at all how I expected to spend the infamous Friday the 13th. I anticipated being at home in the bed, curled up with my kids, eating kettle corn, while watching original thrillers. *What have I gotten myself into?* I wondered as I looked around at the various medical supplies and life-saving equipment inside of the patient transport vehicle.

"My name is Katie," said the energetic and petite EMT that was driving.

Katie's long blonde ponytail looked like it was straight off Rapunzel's head as it extended well past her bottom.

"And you can just call me Toya," said the black EMT with the low faded haircut and lazy eye that sat across from me in a masculine tone.

I listened to the two female EMT's talk about their significant others and their children. I turned my head away from them. Although my eyes were bloodshot red, I still didn't want them to see me cry.

I cried uncontrollably in front of enough people at the hospital and couldn't bear another endless episode. My eyes remained closed as I could only imagine how ridiculous I looked with my arms and legs strapped to the bed like a crazy person, not to mention, the interior lights remained on the entire drive.

My stomach started to drop as I felt the vehicle slowing down, making a series of winding turns. I finally opened my eyes to look at my surroundings. There were medical professionals everywhere. Everyone was just walking and talking, existing happily while my world was in shambles. The sight of blue scrubs began to make me nauseous. I was starving and had nothing to eat or drink all day and the thought of becoming sick again sickened me.

"Are you sure you don't want to use your phone before you go inside?" asked Toya as she released me from the straps.

"I will charge it up when I get situated," I said to her.

There was an awkward silence between the two women. Toya opened the back doors. The cool breeze felt refreshing.

"They didn't tell you that you can't have electronics during your stay for privacy reasons?" she asked me while she held my hand as I stepped out the vehicle.

I was in a total state of shock.

"Do you have a light?" I asked as I removed my Black & Mild cigar from my purse. They shared that awkward look again. Katie pulled a lighter out of her blue scrub pocket.

"Let me guess, I can't smoke here either?" I asked as she released her lighter into the palm of my hand.

"Let's just say you can't take anything you have on you, with you," said Toya.

Katie nudged her in the side and tried to reassure me that it really wasn't that bad, and I should be in and out in no time.

We made small talk and they allowed me time to finish my cigar. I joked about how it was perfect timing getting my hair braided last week as I still had my Senegalese twist in a perfect bun. I knew that no matter how much I procrastinated with them, reality would come sooner than later. I stood in front of the large multi-unit facility surrounded by surveillance cameras, security access doors, gates, and bob-wired fencing. The ladies escorted me to the entrance door and we were let in by facility security. Once we arrived at registration, they parted ways with me, wishing me the best on my journey.

My picture was taken against a neutral colored wall and my body was scanned manually with a hand detector. All the contents of my wallet, including cash and cards, were counted and placed into a transparent plastic bag with an adhesive seal. A picture of the contents was taken. The same procedure was done for my purse and its contents. I had to remove the laces from my shoes and the belt from my pants. Thankfully TJ was already in route to the facility with my personal belongings. I wanted nothing more than to shower and lay down.

I complied with the requisitions and asked for a light snack as I knew that if it wasn't after midnight, it was very close to it. I was guided to the intake room which had a large window, a desk, two chairs opposite from each other, and a television broadcasting the Food Network channel with no remote control. A young lady knocked on the door and brought me a packaged turkey sandwich with mayo, lettuce, and cheese, cut in halves along with a bottle of water, a bottle of apple juice, a package of powdered doughnuts, a bag of graham crackers and a strawberry nutri-grain bar. I was in food heaven as I scuffed down everything but the doughnuts. She came back to the room about ten minutes later with a packaged cup for a urine sample and informed me that it would be followed by blood work, then an assessment shortly afterwards.

My body was cold and tired, and I wanted nothing more than to get the remaining of the process over with so that I could lay down and finally get some rest as the day had been long and tiresome. The assessment consisted of both simple true and false as well as open-ended questions regarding my physical, mental and emotional health history. I was down to the last step of the admission process, and guided to a secure area for a final safety check prior to boarding the female dormitory. The room was empty with the exception of two chairs and a security screen of some sort.

Two black female guards in security uniforms entered the room.

"Remove the bobby pins from your hair and place them in this bag, then step on the other side of that screen and remove your shoes and clothes, including your bra, then stand with your arms and legs spread apart," said one of the guards sternly while the other stood against the wall with her hands coupled together in front of her.

"Are you serious?" I asked shockingly.

"This is standard admittance procedure and no one is exempt," said the other guard.

"No, I will not do it. There are a lot of things *you* people don't initially disclose beforehand. What type of imprisonment is this? You will not violate my rights as if I'm a criminal. I will not strip down to my bare skin and have you invasively search me. I've done no crime and if this is the admit process then I will sign myself right out of here. This was a terrible mistake," I said to both of them as I asked for a phone to call my husband.

The two guards asked me to wait there. The door closed behind them as they stood outside of the room talking amongst each other. I was beyond frustrated and wanted nothing more than to be at home in my bed asleep. When the door opened, the elder of the two guards returned inside.

"Looka here, I could lose my job for this, but I understand what you're saying. I don't necessarily agree with the entire process, but it's in place for a reason as I've seen numerous things firsthand over the many years I've been here. Shoot child, you'd be surprised to find the sharp objects people have hidden under their clothes and even inside of their bodies, and it doesn't always turn out with a happy ending," she said to me.

"Now, we're going to do this quick and easy. I'm going to have you go over there and remove your clothes one piece at a time then pass it to me. I'll check it and hand it right back to you. You can either remove the wires from your bra or go braless. I won't physically search your body, just your clothes, and you better not tell a soul," she said nervously.

I agreed to not utter a word. Needless to say, I wasn't destroying my $60 Victoria Secret bra so I opted to be carefree and let my *girls* catch some wind. It was during my partial search that I realized the other guard was standing outside of the door to ensure no administrative officials were coming since procedure wasn't being followed and disciplinary action could occur.

"Thank you … thank you," I said to her graciously.

After the search, a wrist band with my personal information and my intake mug shot was loosely placed on my left arm. I was led outdoors to enter the female side of what everyone referred to as South, one of the housing facilities aboard. My eyes were red and my face was excessively puffy. I was given a blanket, a pillow, two towels, a blue scrub set, and some toiletries. I asked the receptionist on the floor about my belongings that TJ brought and was reassured that I would receive them first thing in the morning as they had to go through a security check first. She placed a bright red wristband on my right arm along with a green band and a yellow band on my left arm. I had no clue what the colors represented and was too fatigued to inquire.

There were daily schedules posted throughout the hallways. The halls were quiet as most of the women were asleep. I was taken to my sleeping headquarters. The sound of snoring filled the room as tears filled my eyes. *What am I doing here? Is this really where I need to be?* I pondered. Inside the room there were two large viewless windows, three twin sized beds lined up against the neutral colored right wall, three built-in wall cubbies on the left wall, and a bathroom with a walk-in shower and a toilet. There was no door to the bathroom, only a curtain, and the sink was in the sleeping area.

The unoccupied bed was on the end next to the window. There were free phones that resembled old-school pay phones lined up in a row outside of the room, but they were off until the morning. I wrapped up in my blanket and laid down onto the cold, firm bed. There were no clocks, no television, and no way for me to write as pens were prohibited. I buried my face into my pillow as I wanted nothing more than to wake up and be at home.

The next morning, I was awakened by the noise of my dorm mates moving around the room.

"What time is it?" I asked as I rolled over onto my side then quickly back over.

"You didn't read the schedule? Showers are at seven every single morning," said a vibrant young woman name Jazzy who was putting on her bra as she hummed beautifully. She was bi-racial, drop dead gorgeous and couldn't have been any older than eighteen. Her comb easily glided back and forth through her wet curly hair.

"How long have you been here?" I asked her curiously.

"It'll be two weeks Sunday. It's not paradise but it beats living on the streets. Plus, I've made a lot of new friends. I tried to commit suicide by cutting my wrists, but I'm much better now," she said smiling nervously as she pulled down her sleeves to cover the bandaged wounds.

"Monday I will be moving to the apartment housing and I can't wait. You can have your phone, they take you back and forth to therapy and you can go outside and everything!" she added excitingly.

"That's great. I hope it works out for you. I'm going back to bed," I said as I put the cover over my head.

"Attention women, please line up at the medication window for your morning meds" said a loud raspy voice over the intercom.

"Okay, I'm up alright!" I yelled to the ceiling as I threw the cover off my body.

The thought of showering and putting on the same dirty clothes annoyed me. My dorm mates went to line up for their vitals and meds while I contemplated showering and putting on the unflattering blue scrub set. I stepped outside of the room to find that not only were all the phones *still* being utilized, but the lines for medication and vitals both were endlessly wrapped around the entire floor. A fight almost broke out at the water fountain as one lady tripped and spilled her

Dixie cup of water onto the back of the woman ahead of her. Luckily, security intervened before any fists were thrown.

I didn't take medications prior to coming here, so missing the "med" call made no difference to me. I was on strike and ready to rebel against anything they asked of me until I received my personal belongings and dared someone to take action as I was still traumatized from the unethical check-in process. The wait for receiving my stuff was beyond ridiculous as it had been well over seven hours and no one seemed to know anything regarding the delay.

The more time began to pass, the more I felt like this was an incarceration. "Breakfast call" sounded at approximately 8:30am and the women ran, pushed and shoved to get to the cafeteria. I was in no mood for early morning drama, so I waited until some of the foot traffic died down. As I walked down the hall I was abruptly stopped by a braless white chick with meth teeth who lifted up her scrub top to expose her small naked breasts as she flickered her tongue insisting that I wanted some of what she had, before she ran off laughing hysterically.

Before I could make it to the end of the hall in route to the cafeteria, I was stopped again, but this time by a staff member carrying a stack of Styrofoam compartment plates.

"Williams?" he asked.

I nodded in agreement and he verified my armband. He handed me a foam plate then proceeded to walk off. Rude.

"Hey! What is this?" I called out to him.

He turned around. "Red bands can't leave the floor … suicidal," he said as he walked off.

Suicidal? I thought to myself. This must be some sort of mistake.

I walked back to the room and opened the plate as my stomach still hungered and groaned loudly.

"Yuck!" I said as I visually critiqued the meal, almost immediately closing the flimsy container.

The oatmeal and grits were unappealing as they merged together from the commute upstairs. The toast was hard and burnt. Being I'm not really big on pork, I opted to skip the two slices of country ham, though it was the only thing that appeared to be digestible. *No butter or sugar! Who eats like this?* I thought aloud as I tossed the container into the trash.

I walked outside the dorm room and grabbed a small aluminum-foil sealed apple juice container from the community fridge, you know the juices they had in elementary school free lunches. I plopped down on the leather sofa in the sitting area and this was as quiet as I've seen this place since I'd awakened. There were crayons and crossword puzzles scattered across the wood tables and patient drawings hung throughout the walls of the level. I searched around for a clock but there was not one in plain sight. It wasn't before long that the rowdy bunch of ladies began to return from breakfast. Most of the women were comfortable with one another and had the routine down packed.

A line began forming by the door labeled "Group Therapy Room A". I returned to my sleeping headquarters as I had no plans on attending therapy or anything asked of me. I pulled the cover over my eyes and drowned out the chaos around me, along with the things that were beyond my control. It was over twelve hours and I was still being given the run-arounds regarding my personal belongings.

"Aren't you coming?" asked Jazzy as she ran back into the room like a bolt of lightning to grab her blanket.

"No, I'm going to sit this one out," I told her.

"You do know if you don't participate they will keep you longer. They keep track of everything. If you want to get out of here fast, just tell them exactly what they want to hear," she said to me before she jetted out the door.

The session was already in progress as I attempted to tip-toe inside unnoticed. Apparently, there was a story already in progress as all eyes were immediately on me.

"Excuse me, excuse me," I said repeatedly as I made my way to one of three remaining seats in the middle of the largely formed circle.

There were death stares along with some laughter as I adjusted my oversize scrubs. The instructor, Judy, introduced herself and thanked me for joining the group as well as went over the rules of her class and how to get credit for attendance. Jazzy gave me a quick smile then continued to console the young woman next to her. As instructed, I told the group my name and informed them that I wasn't ready to share, just there to listen.

I pleaded with myself to not show emotion as it can be taken as a sign of weakness, but when these women began to open up and speak their own truths, I couldn't help but empathize with the pains that filled the room. From rape and molestation, prostitution and homelessness, to physical abuse and substance abuse. There were so many warriors and overcomers. While many of the women saw themselves as purposeless and defeated, I saw them as inspirational and testimonial. Out of the darkness comes light, and I could see their inner dimensions. I could feel the energy from the strength and courage they possessed, and as I wept for them, I prayed for each one of them to find capacity within.

As the boxes of tissue were being passed around the room, I raised my hand to share with the group as I dried my eyes.

"So, what brought you here?" asked Judy as she stood in the center of the circle with her back strait and palms relaxed.

I took a deep breath and exhaled as I looked around the room to see that all attention was centered on me. There was a quick tap on the door. Judy apologized to me as she got up to open the door. She stepped outside of the room and swiftly reentered.

"Your doctor is ready to see you. We'll pick up tomorrow if you're feeling up to sharing with the group. Thank you for coming," she said to me with a warm smile holding the door ajar. The ladies all told me "goodbye" as I exited.

I walked out of the room and was led by my assigned psychiatrist, Dr. Lee.

Dr. Lee was in what appeared to be his early fifties and of Asian ethnicity. We spent about twenty minutes going over what primarily led to my intake at the facility. I was as open and honest with him as I could be, and I dared to not play the victim, admitting to my own faults and flaws within the marriage. As he listened, he encouraged me to go deeper … to go back as far as I could remember the initial sadness and emptiness starting.

I apologized for my emotions over and over again and he reassured me that not only was I very much sane and competent, what I was experiencing and feeling were very normal reactions to the trauma I've endured over the years. As our time came to an ending, I believe that he still knew that I was barely scratching the surface of the pain.

"We'll continue our session tomorrow. I'm moving you to another housing facility—The Sailing. There you will be with more functional and working adults like yourself. You won't have to hear the traumatic rape and abuse stories … just good working people who are going through some tough times, many of which I'm sure you'll be able to relate to. I'm confident that you'll like it much better over there. I'll also be prescribing you some night medications to help you rest and some trial dosages of meds for the depression," Dr. Lee said to me before shaking my hand and escorting me out of his office.

I was in a state of panic as I was being moved and still didn't have my belongings, but I dared not lash out and end up with more time added to my sentence. Lunchtime came and went and the ladies began to line up for dinner. I called TJ as often as I could and he welcomed my every call, steadily apologizing for me even being there. I sat in solitude on my bed looking at the wall for hours as I wanted nothing more than to shower and smoke my Black & Mild.

I heard a cart rolling down the hall. There was a knock on the door and I eagerly welcomed the visitor. There were two care givers asking me to inspect my list of belongings and ensure it matched the contents delivered. I was so happy to see my robe, undies, pajamas, books and personal hygiene products. There was a sealed box of Black & Mild regular cigars, due to the *wine* flavor being strangely prohibited.

While the thought of smoking regular Blacks normally sickened me, I couldn't wait to fire it up and take a few puffs.

"Are you ready?" asked one of the care givers.

"They're ready for you in the other wing. I'll give you two minutes to gather your things," she added as she handed me two large brown paper sacks and then stood outside the door.

I felt an anxiety attack coming but I tried my best to maintain my calmness. I didn't even get a chance to say goodbye to Jazzy or the others as I was finally coming out of my shell and warming up to them. My red wristband was finally removed from my arm. As we walked across the corridor, with my bags crammed into my arms, I could taste the freshness of the cool air. I had taken so many things for granted and being here was putting everything into perspective.

From the time I stepped foot inside of The Sailing facility, it was a totally different ambiance than that of South. Samantha, the resident advisor, warmly greeted us and gave me a branded water bottle and fleece blanket. She escorted me to my room, giving me a tour of the facility along the way. Each room slept two women, although there were a few single rooms which were of course "occupied". There were cordless phones, a business center with computers and the internet, a fitness center, and there was even a serenity garden where you could go outside and walk or just sit and admire the scenery.

When we arrived at the designated dorm room, the door was pulled up. Samantha knocked gently before slightly pushing the door ajar. I was in awe at the oversize walk-in closet in the room and the adjustable thermostat units, unlike South. There was a young, petite, adorable white girl wrapped in an oversize University of Memphis towel brushing her long blonde hair in the mirror.

"Hi!" she said to me with a pleasant smile.

Samantha introduced me to Casey. I told Casey that I would give her some privacy to get dressed as I honestly just wanted to smoke. Besides, the room was hot and steamy from the shower and it was suffocating me.

Samantha directed me to the smoking areas.

"Do you have a light?" I asked her.

She laughed and assured me that she didn't smoke and then explained to me how to use the in-ground flameless lighter. After several failed attempts of getting a strong light, a middle-aged white man approached me, offering to light my cigar as he saw my struggle. I was a little hesitant at first, then graciously allowed him to do so as he introduced himself to me as Gary. He had a strong career with the printing press business and he was knowledgeable. Gary was very talkative, but a pleasure to listen to as there was so much passion within him about getting his life back on track.

I was honestly just thrilled to be in the presence of an adult that I could relate to, let alone it being a male without it being a punishable offense. I was yelled at on the other wing for interacting with male patients as two young black guys were trying to hit on me while I was transferring units and I simply informed them of my lack of interest. As a result, I was verbally scolded by one of the guards for interacting with the male patients. I mean who tries to hook up with someone they met in a mental institution? You don't know why I'm here or what personal issues I'm dealing with.

As I inhaled and exhaled my cigar, it just felt good to be outside at my own free will. While I was still enclosed by metal bars, I knew that my circumstances were only temporary. I finally was able to understand that being here is just part of the journey and to not reject the experience, but to embrace it, own it, and learn from it. The temperature outside began to drop drastically. Gary and I shivered as we continued our conversation. His presence was appreciated.

"Come on, let's go inside and have some hot cocoa," Gary said to me.

Gary made me some hot cocoa in the Keurig in the recreation area. He filled his water bottle with crushed ice and acai-pomegranate flavored water from the 24-hour beverage station. It was late, but we enjoyed each other's company. We talked until they called the men and women to line up separately at the designated medication stations. The charge nurse on duty verified our identity, followed by a cross-check of our prescribed meds before distribution. Once verified, she had a glass pitcher filled with ice water and small Dixie cups waiting to be filled. Afterwards, she visually inspected our mouths to ensure all meds were properly consumed.

After my first dose of meds, I could simultaneously feel the sleep coming on heavily. I walked back to my room. Casey was lying in her bed in an oversized college sweatshirt with matching cotton bottoms, cuddled up in her facility branded fleece blanket. The room was still humid from her shower, but it was nippy outside, so I appreciated the extra warmth.

Casey had a ton of books with her and she appeared to be studying for her college courses. I opted to not bother her although she did strike up some small talk, informing me she'd be leaving in two days. I told her about my experience at the South facility thus far and she empathized. She showed me how to work the shower and allowed me to use her travel sized body wash as they confiscated the full-size bottle that TJ brought to me.

As the near scorching water poured onto my naked body, I couldn't help but miss singing and rock star jamming in the shower to my favorite tunes. Nevertheless, I humbly reminded myself of the blessing it was to not only be able to finally take a shower in a bathroom with a real door, but to be in a facility where I could actually get some treatment for my depression and not feel like an inmate. I needed the discipline that came along with being on this unit. I finished my shower, brushed my teeth and laid in my bed awake.

"Do you like to write?" asked Casey from across the room.

"Love too!" I replied back eagerly.

She got out of her bed and went to her side of the walk-in closet and gave me a composition book and an adult coloring book.

"And here you go," she said perky as she tossed me a couple of colored pencils and ink pens.

"How'd you get these?" I asked puzzled since I knew they were prohibited items.

"My boyfriend brings me whatever I want every day," she said to me.

"How is it that you see him every day?"

"Girl we can have visitors each day at 5:45p.m. for forty-five minutes and on the weekend for an hour in the afternoon," she said to me. "Jake stays on campus too, so he just drives here every day. It's not too bad of a drive. Besides, I always make it worth the drive," she said smiling as she started back reading her anatomy book.

"If I start snoring, wake me up!" I warned her.

"It's okay…I'll probably be snoring louder than you," she joked.

I turned towards the wall and opened the composition notebook. All I saw was pages and pages of instant relief as my estrogen levels rose. When I picked up the pen, my thoughts were all over the place and I didn't know where to start, but I figured the best place to start was from the heart. There was nothing but me and my thoughts, with no interruptions, so I seized the moment and mentally released some tension…

Never been so depressed in all my life.
Don't know which way to turn so I keep it all inside.
The weight of the world seems to be on my shoulder.
Sometimes I feel like I should just go on and get it over.
The love for my kids is what keeps me going.
To hold them in my arms my heart is longing.
Seven long years is what I gave to this man.
All hopes and dreams shattered to whereas you'd never understand.
The complexity of the marriage was even hard for me to comprehend.
Countless affairs and sleepless nights.
While smiling for the world pretending everything was alright.
Trips to the Keys and cruising overseas.
Not realizing that for his heart I had to compete.

Pride gone and self-esteem depleted.
Catering to a man so selfish and conceited.
Intelligent, beautiful, and a heart full of love.
Yet lying habitually with no regrets of.
Praying to God to restore and make us stronger.
Dying on the inside cause I couldn't take it any longer.
So many games, way too many lies.
So much pain, way too many cries.
When we made love all I saw was you and her.
So many unanswered questions, so much I needed to know.
Whenever you needed me I was at your beck and call.
Screw up after screw up, I would never let you fall.
Still selfishness and greed made you destroy it all.
When you lay down with dogs you wake up with fleas.
Now here you are saying "baby please."
Marriage is supposed to be full of joy and peace.
Your spouse should be your best friend to say the least.
A relationship built off love and trust.
A bond that can't be destroyed by adulterated lust.
I could write pages, hell, probably a whole book.
But at the end of the day, it won't change what you took.

The next morning, I awoke to Samantha opening the door and turning on the lights, telling all the ladies it was time to make beds and shower.

"Nooo!" Casey cried as she buried her head into her pillow.

"What's wrong?" I asked.

"Ugh … Samantha kept me up all night as she came into the room to check on us every fifteen freaking minutes, shining that damn bright flashlight in my face. She takes her role way too serious and she's the only one of *them* who does that," she complained as she turned back over, ignoring her call to get up.

It was then that I was informed about the tale of the patient who suffocated herself to death one night and no one found her until the next morning. Knowing that, I appreciated the safety checks, especially at a place like this. I, on the other hand, slept beautifully after I took my meds and poured my heart into words. I heard no door opening nor did I see any bright lights. I put on my ultra-bright pink plush robe and slipper socks and headed out for a morning smoke.

Even though I'd stayed two nights already, this was what felt like my first "official" day. I was even oddly excited as Dr. Lee has a session with me later to go over the best drug and non-drug treatment options for my post-care plan. Immediately following the morning meds, we had our first meeting of the day. There was a total of sixteen of us, at least initially, with the women outnumbering the men. Amongst us was a stunning local journalist, an educator, a government worker, a college student, a wealth-inherited college drop-out, a beautician, and even an atheist to name a few.

The group was very diverse racially, professionally, and socioeconomically. Everyone seemed to hang out in their own little small groups or cliques. Everyone except for the atheist, Linda. No one welcomed her and while the thought of not believing in a deity is too much for my brain to even process, she was still a human being and she was being treated noticeably different. I sympathized for her, but I longed for the likeness and acceptance more, so I turned a blind eye to the discrimination.

The community meeting was short and sweet as it was primarily to welcome "new patients" to the group and go over the rules and requirements, along with the daily schedule and what's mandated. Afterwards, both male and female patients all lined up to travel to the South building for breakfast. Everyone appeared to be nice and welcomed me with opened arms. I knew I still looked like an emotional wreck, but my reality was that I would never have to see any of these people ever again. So for once in my life, I was free to be me and not worry or care about other's perception of me. A part of me was dreading breakfast as thinking about the stiff oatmeal and grits gave me chills.

The moment we stepped foot inside of the cafeteria, the smell of French toast filled the air. We were the only group of patients down there and we were urged to finish in a timely manner as the raucous South patients would be coming in right behind us. There were so many options to choose from. They had bagels with cream cheeses, yogurts, fruits, hot and cold cereals, along with a full hot breakfast bar. I opted for the French toast slices with syrup, turkey sausage links, and fresh fruit, along with iced apple juice for my beverage.

Once I filled my tray with my likings, I felt like the new girl in high school on her first day in the cafeteria as I stood front and centered looking for a clique to accept me. A hand from across the room motioned for me to come and join the table. I took a deep breath as I proceeded with stereotypical caution to the table with only black women. There were six chairs, four of which were occupied.

The ladies introduced themselves to me as Winter, Rochelle, Angelina, and Phyllis. None of their names matched their faces. I looked around the cafeteria for Casey, but I wasn't surprised to see that she was socializing with the people who she identified best with. Hell, at the end of the day could I really blame her or any of us for sticking to what we know in a place like this?

Out of nowhere ran up a distressed white girl with shoulder length black hair and glasses. She sat down at the last empty seat and the women anticipated her presence.

"What did they say?" whispered one of the girls to her.

"I can't even talk about it right now. I need to leave. I don't need to be here right now," she said panicking as she lifted her eyeglasses to wipe her running mascara and her tears.

Her name is Allie and she's a beautician and make-up artist. Allie is in her mid-to-late twenties, about 5'6" and has some serious junk in the trunk for a white girl. Although I didn't know what was wrong with her, I definitely could feel her energy and her spirit very strongly, and her pain saddened me.

After breakfast there was a morning meditation session consisting of thirty minutes of inhale and exhale breathing exercises on yoga mats along with light stretching to a voice-guided instructor. Immediately following that was a mandatory process therapy group session. The topic of the physician-led therapy session was "emotion regulation skills", and while it seemed like basic, elementary principles, it's always easier said than done.

Whenever we experience an emotion, it is typically followed by a behavior. We were encouraged to do the opposite action to help change our extreme emotions. I was used as an example as I openly admitted to the group that when I'm angry or despondent, I tend to stick to myself and oftentimes shut down completely. The instructor suggested that instead of me emotionally withdrawing, next time I experience emotions of anger or sadness, I should instead try to communicate openly about my feelings or even visit some friends to keep from sheltering myself. He stated that in doing so I will not only get to the underlying reason as to what triggered my emotion, but I will then be able to differentiate if my emotion and its intensity match the facts of the situation.

Listening to everyone's emotional stories was mentally exhausting. I just wanted to rest my eyes for a few moments, but the day was packed with back to back prescheduled "activities". It was hard for me to comprehend that it was lunch time already. *Like how could anyone be hungry so soon?* We had breakfast only four hours ago and my body is not used to eating that close together, so I hadn't built up an appetite.

I skipped lunch, although it looked delicious as it had a picnic style theme. They had hamburgers, hot dogs, cole slaw, corn on the cob and vanilla cake with coconut frosting for dessert, and let's not mention a salad bar with the works. They even had cheese and pepperoni pizza slices as an alternative option! I sat at the table with the ladies and the six of us conversed openly. It's sad to say that a man was at the root of every woman's reason for being there.

Winter is a single-mom with a young son struggling to be with a man who is torn between her and the mother of his other children. He admits to being in love with them both and neither of them are willing to let him go.

Angelina, not sure why she has a Spanish name, has this uncontrollable desire to fit in. She paints herself to be helpless in her role as a wife and mother, then boasts about how spoiled her husband has her because she's so good to him. She desperately craves attention and desires to be the center of attention at all times. She says that she experiences severe anxiety and depression … frequently.

Rochelle is an engaged mother of four who's getting married in less than a month. Her fiancé-to-be, whom she has no children with, cheated on her, she retaliated, and now they are at that dark place where they don't trust each other. Not to mention, throw post-partum depression into the mix. She's not even sure if she'll make it down the aisle at this point.

Phyllis is fresh out of college and has already landed a career in her dream field of theatre. She is eccentric and intelligent but has commitment issues along with some social skills that need attention.

Finally, Allie the beautician, is a wife and mother of two to a military spouse. She and her husband have fallen out of love and desperately want to rekindle, but there is someone new in her life and the stress from the marriage and affair is heavy on her.

I listened quietly as they spoke and reassured them that they were not alone and being in this season was all a part of their journey and the best way through it is to learn to embrace it, although I knew its difficulty.

After lunch there was a second process therapy group meeting. This meeting was much lengthier than the first as it was more personal. The meeting was about "interpersonal effectiveness skills" and as with any session, active participation is the key element in being released from the facility. The confirmed average length of stay is five to seven days and while I found participating in the discussions to be therapeutically comforting, I couldn't bear the thought of being away from the outside world that long. I missed my children, my phone, my high-stress job, and my comfort zone … my TJ.

After the session ended, we had recreational activity time. Although breezy, the weather was pleasant, so the group proceeded to the outdoor trail for a nature walk. The circular trail extended about a half of mile in total length. There was a breath-taking lake with a fountain in the center. Trees, flowers and benches were amidst the flawless landscaping. We stood on the bridge, overlooking the amazing scenery and admiring its simplicity.

The sixteen of us broke apart into our own divided cliques. We collectively walked the trail three times before proceeding back. From there we played ping-pong and foosball indoors to pass the remaining of the time, and for the first time in an unfortunate long time, I found myself truly enjoying myself. I was doing what I wanted to do, and it felt good doing just that. I didn't care about how pathetic I looked or the skills that I lacked, I was just enjoying being outside of my comfort zone and being carefree.

There was a brief period of downtime afterwards, followed by a bipolar seminar and a trauma seminar. I was relieved that my presence wasn't mandated at those events as I was honestly just exhausted. I haven't had a schedule that intense since my initial on the job training and wanted nothing more than to relax as the day was creeping away. I called TJ and talked to my kids as often as I could without them actually knowing where I was, but my absence was definitely causing an uproar on the home-front. I knew that I needed to get back to my warzone as this was a tropical oasis in comparison.

When I arrived back to the dorm, Casey wasn't there and for the first time since being at the facility, I had some *me* time. I was overwhelmed with emotion and wanted to seize the moment as I knew the bipolar seminar was scheduled for an hour and a half, followed by visitation then dinner. While I didn't have the candles, music or wine that I so heartily desired, I turned off the lights, closed the lockless door and openly undressed while letting a hot shower run.

I missed being touched. TJ was in route for visitation and I wasn't sure if I was feeling apprehension or anxiousness. I fantasized about how it would be when I got discharged. Hell, I fantasized about how it would be later that day. *Would I welcome his advances, or would bitterness still be at the root of every touch?* I wrapped my long Nubian braids in a large bath towel then entered the shower slowly, singing softly as I lathered my body in suds. I felt like a caged bird seeking its rightful freedom, knowing which way to go to escape, just too afraid to fly to the new horizons that await, too afraid of the unknown and unseen.

My thoughts were interrupted by a loud intercom message specifically requesting *my* mandatory attendance in Therapy Room C. I hated how they called my full name so loudly as if I wanted everyone to know who I was. I jumped out of the shower and dressed as quickly as I could out of fear they would make a second announcement if I wasn't walking through the door at any second. I found myself running down the hallway until I heard some giggles behind me. I stopped dead in my tracks and turned around only to see the two women who were snickering cease.

I turned back around to proceed to my destination until I realized my braids weren't slapping me across my back while I ran. I touched my head and my braids were still wrapped in the towel.

"Silly tricks!" I said as I thought back to their elementary laughter. I quickly took the towel off my head and made a detour to the laundry room to toss it. Before I could exit, a secondary announcement was being made along with a two-minute warning. While I wondered the consequences for the severity of my tardiness, I also knew that I had human rights and would threaten to call a lawyer in a heartbeat if I was to get more time added simply from showering during downtime.

My heart raced fast as I approached the door. I could only imagine what type of awkward setting I was walking into late. I exhaled deeply, then forcefully swung the door open, hoping my portrayal of being in a bad mood would make people automatically back off. I looked around the empty, mini-conference room and saw Dr. Lee sitting at the opposite end of the long oblong table. He instructed me to have a seat near him.

Before I could ask what this was all about, the door opened and his face lit up in great delight as he motioned the tall, slender African-American woman towards us.

"Rachel, so good to see you," he said to her as they shook hands professionally.

Young, beautiful and successful. Just the inspiration I need, I thought sarcastically to myself as he introduced me to Dr. Riley—an onsite psychologist.

Dr. Lee explained to me that Dr. Riley will perform a brief psychological assessment and then *they* will determine if I'm on the best medication or if medication is even needed.

Dr. Lee excused himself from the room and told her that he'd be back in about thirty minutes. *So much for my me time*, I thought as I sighed aloud. I folded my arms across my chest as she talked to me about her educational background and love for her profession.

Horrible ice breaking/introductory skills, I thought as I laughed under my breath.

"Is there something funny?" she asked in a serious tone as she removed her thin framed, naughty girl glasses.

"I just don't see how any of this is relevant or helping me," I expressed honestly.

She sat her stack of papers aside, clasped her hands together on the table and made eye contact with me.

"Fair enough. Tell me why you feel like you're here," she said to me.

I knew that she had access to my admittance information, so I wasn't sure if she was asking me this out of arrogance, ignorance or purely just to hear it in my own words. I knew that time was money and I didn't have the money to waste *her* time, so I decided to give her the benefit of the doubt and tickle her fancy.

"Well, I'm here because I feel I have very little self-control over my emotions and it's detrimental. Sometimes I feel like I'm just stuck ... just consciously redreaming the same nightmare and being too afraid to awaken from it. For as long as I can remember, I've had this desire to be loved by any means, ignoring the most transparent of signs. I'm very intuitive and have always been extremely sensitive. Not just Disney, Lifetime movie sensitive, but every little and not so little thing. Weddings, funerals, sports, Feed the Need commercials, arguments, and the list goes on and on," I said to her.

"Can you recall a time when you felt brave because you were in total control of your emotions?" she asked me.

I thought for a moment then smiled as I shook my head no.

"Why did you smile before acknowledging you *didn't* remember?"

"Because it's irrelevant as it was long ago and talking about it will change nothing."

"Well, I care about what you have to say, and I would love for you to share it with me. Nothing is too silly or too long ago."

"Look ma'am, with all due respect, I've had issues with men *and* myself as far back as I can remember ... as far back as when my sister died and that was in ninety-seven. I can't remember the last time I felt whole."

"Were you close to your sister?"

I wondered what kind of question that was as we were both two little girls growing up in the same home, being raised by the same parents, not even two whole years apart in age.

"She was my true best friend. Even though I feel that way in my heart, the guilt of never seizing that moment to express my love to her still breaks me down. My sister looked up to me and wanted to be around me 24/7. There were so many times that I was so mean to her and chose my then best friend over her. I question if my sister even knows I love her."

"How did she pass away if you don't mind my asking?"

I did mind her inquiring very much and my mood was quickly shifting to irritable and uncomfortable as I rubbed my forearm back and forth.

"She died in a car wreck."

"Were you there?"

"Yes."

"You said it was 1997, do you remember the exact day?"

"It was a Friday morning. I wore a black long-sleeve bodysuit with a pair of loosely fitted denim jeans and my braids were up in a high ponytail. Is that *exact* enough?"

"Yes, very good. You have a great memory. Now I want you to close your eyes and with mental clarity, focus and travel back in time to that Friday morning. When you get there, I want you to step outside of *you* and walk me through what you see, as if you were watching it on TV."

I contemplated whether or not I wanted to share with her and before I could consciously conclude, I found myself randomly rambling, or should I say venting.

"You know, it's funny the depth of the things we remember. I can vividly remember my first day of pre-kindergarten. I cried the entire day as I had never been away from my mom and thankfully it was only half days, as that literally continued for the entire first two weeks. Fast-forward three years later, I can remember the bus breaking down on our way to a farm field trip. As always, my mom chaperoned and tried to lift my spirits being all the other kids were outside playing games to pass the time. I, on the other hand, cried the entire time. I'll never forget how all the kids circled around me laughing while singing 'Sally Walker' while I cried to myself."

I paused for a moment, although it was too late to stop as I could feel the adrenaline rush from the release. Dr. Riley nodded for me to continue. I closed my eyes and exhaled deeply.

"Now, let's fast-forward four years later. Let's go to March 7, 1997. That was the day that changed my life forever. My two sisters and

I woke up for school as we did every morning. We lived in a small three-bedroom brick house in the impoverished Boxtown area in Memphis. My mom made us oatmeal with fresh apples and raisins as she prepared a hot meal every day before and after school. We were running behind schedule so none of us were able to finish eating. My mom hadn't long gotten in from work, but she still got us ready and off to school.

"My parents had a 1990 light blue, Ford Taurus at the time. It was the newest car we'd ever owned. This particular day, I sat in the front seat. My youngest sister sat behind me and my eldest sister sat behind my mother. My younger sister and I typically would fight over who rides in the front seat, but that day, she gave me the front seat without any questions asked. My oldest sister never cared about the front seat. We all got inside of the car, but it wasn't until it was too late that I discovered that I was the only person wearing a seatbelt.

"We were about two blocks away from our school when our vehicle was struck by an oncoming car. I can still hear the screams in my head. The electrical pole fell and crushed the back end of our car. I can remember unbuckling my seat belt, turning towards my mother and older sister as they laid there, eyes closed and motionless, while blood ran from my baby sister's face, in my heart knowing she was gone as the electrical pole smashed in the back passenger side. I can remember just not knowing what to do as people where running from every direction to try to help. From regular civilians to medical professionals who were driving and pulled over to assist. There was so much chaos.

"The doors were jammed and emergency responders had to remove my mother and sisters. There was blood. There was a lot of blood. 'I have a pulse!' yelled the paramedic giving my baby sister CPR, planting seeds of hope in our hearts, in my heart. Within what seemed like mere minutes, a helicopter landed and airlifted my youngest sister to Le Bonheur Children's Hospital. The ambulance transported the three of us to The Med Hospital as we continued to hold onto hope.

"Needless to say, it wasn't long after we got there that they announced she died on the way to the hospital. Words cannot begin to describe the pain and devastation my parents, my family suffered from such a great lost. Both my older sister and mother were left with countless broken and fractured bones while I miraculously walked away from that deadly wreck without a single scratch. But you know the part that gets me the most is that I never cried. From the time I learned her death was confirmed all the way to the day she was laid to rest, I didn't cry.

"I can remember walking back into that house for the first time after she passed away. It was so lonely and so cold in there, almost as if the home was foreign to me. Our bowls of hardened oatmeal were still in the same exact spot as were our scattered Barbie dolls and cassette tapes. I remember walking to the closet that we shared and closing my eyes as I smelled our matching brand-new dresses we tried on the night before her death. One dress was bright red and the other was dark blue and they were made from some shimmery, bouncy material. My sister wanted the red dress and even though the red dress was shorter and I was taller, somehow, I convinced my mom that it should be mine, and it was. I laughed at how silly I was and wished that merely giving it to her would bring her back, but I knew it wouldn't. I vowed to let her be buried in the red dress that she loved so much, and in return I would wear the dark blue dress to her funeral.

"I didn't know where my unprecedented strength came from, but I just recall rising to the occasion and reassuring my parents that it was not their fault, it was an accident, and our family would be okay. We didn't have money and needless to say, no insurance of any kind, so an untimely death of such made it financially unaffordable to provide a proper burial. My parents had to seek financial assistance from my mother's side of the family, many of whom still to this day despise my father for the emotional turmoil he put my mother through.

"My sister was buried five days after her death, which out of spite, was held on our father's 39th birthday. It's crazy how I'll never forget that because we were Muslim, the reverend at my mother's family church didn't even allow the obituaries inside the church. It was then when I began to see the true darkness of the world. As heartbreaking as it was, my parents weren't granted permission to distribute the obituaries until after the service ended. I cried the entire funeral, from start to finish, but I still felt brave," I said to her.

Dr. Riley looked at me and gave me a warm smile. An unfamiliar sense of relief came across me.

"You are very strong and you have, and from what I hear, always had a lot of fight in you. While I may not know exactly what led up to you being here, I do know a fighter when I come across one and I'm saying this because this is true," she said to me.

There was a quick knock on the door, followed by Dr. Lee's earlier than anticipated entrance.

"You're definitely not crazy and I'll pass my documentations along to Dr. Lee so that he can adjust your medication appropriately. I will also pass your psychological results along to your doctor when she returns tomorrow."

"Whoa! Wait … what? Did I miss something here? Are you not a psychologist?"

"I am, just not *your* assigned psychologist. However, Dr. Keaton is your doctor and she's great as she has extensive experience dealing with patients who have had traumatic events to occur in their lives. You're a champion and you will be fine," Dr. Riley said to me before we parted ways.

A part of me felt betrayed as I shared some of the most intimate details of my personal life with her, a person I didn't even know a half an hour ago. Most people don't press the issue when I say I lost my sister, but I allowed myself to deceptively become subjective to vulnerability. I've never been asked to or even considered reliving the experience, although I admit that it felt painfully soothing. It was almost as if I found the answer to the questions that I've pondered for so long. I experienced a very tough loss at a young age and I blamed myself, not for her leaving the physical realm, but for me not genuinely having shown my love. As a result, I've tried to hold onto everything and everyone, despite the level of toxicity.

I learned how to deal with things by not dealing with them at an early age as my mother never complained about anything, no matter how bad things were physically or financially. I admit that I grew up as a daddy's girl and in my eyes, daddy could do no wrong. My maternal grandmother despised and chastised me for it. My father was very involved with disciplining us and keeping us grounded when we were young girls, and I will be forever gracious for it. Nevertheless, as I grew into a teenager, I took my 3D glasses off and saw things for what they really were. I saw the pain, struggle and fatigue in my mother from my father's physical, spiritual and financial absence. While there is no remembrance of major physical abuse, the mental and emotional took its toll on her, on all of us.

When I made it back to the room, Casey was already back from the seminar she attended as it dismissed earlier than scheduled. I noticed that she had on a pair of black leggings as she was brushing her hair in the mirror, again. It's ironic because several of the "curvier" women, including myself, leggings and spandex clothing items did not make it pass security check. I didn't care enough to put up a fight as I knew I'd be leaving soon and so was she.

"I'm so excited! I get to see my boyfriend. Are you having any visitors today?" Casey asked me.

"Yeah, my husband is actually coming here to see me. It'll be the first time since my stay as I didn't know visitation was every day. I'm a bit nervous because it's been a rough few years."

"I definitely get that. I'm here because I've just been super depressed since my parents got a divorce. My daddy said I was taking it hard and I needed help. Some of his dental colleagues recommended the facility, so here I am!"

"Oh, I'm so sorry to hear about your parent's divorce," I said to her in a somewhat sarcastic tone.

While I felt that *my* problems were bigger than hers, I knew that there were people out there, just feet away from me, with problems way deeper than mine, so I ceased my vain judgment immediately.

When I saw TJ for the first time, it was calming to be in his familiar presence. I don't know what I would've done if they hadn't called my name for having a visitor as it made me feel loved, wanted and missed. We hugged one another as if a lifetime had passed. We sat down at the table, adjacent from each other and had casual conversation as there was so much to say, yet so little time. Furthermore, this was not the time nor place for us to go in depth about the reality of where we stood.

We looked around and saw couples embracing one another, parents consoling their adult children, friends pacifying their loved ones … we looked around and we saw love. It was one of the most visually captivating sights. Without words, we chose to enjoy the forty-five minutes that we shared talking about his work, the kids, upcoming plans and so forth. I envisioned it being painful and awkward, but it turned out to be quite gratifying. I looked across the room at Casey who was cuddled up in her boyfriend's lap. I smiled at her and she gave me a sly grin. TJ asked me what that was about, and I simply informed him that she was my roommate and I shared no details with her or any of the women for that matter, about *our* private matters.

As the conversation continued with ease, the two of us had forgotten that time was of the essence as a "two-minutes remaining" announcement was made by one of the supervising guards. Several of the patients were still trying to conceal their newly acquired goodies and other prohibited items before they exited the visitation room. Although I didn't anticipate being there much longer, I saw how easy it was for outside things to be brought in as security officials only checked visitor's belongings, not their physical body. I mean, I didn't want any narcotics or razors, but I did want a box of Black & Mild *wine* flavored cigars and some banana flavored Now-and-Laters. TJ vowed to return with them tomorrow at the "same time, same place". We shared a laugh at his corny comment, then he gave me a handful of folded small bills as the vending machines on the unit only accepts ones and gives no change back. The two remaining minutes flew by and before we knew it, we kissed, hugged and parted ways.

I was mentally exhausted as I played in my fried chicken and macaroni & cheese at dinner. I did however enjoy a salad with the works, topped off with a balsamic vinaigrette dressing. I can truly say I'd been eating much healthier and consistently since being there. I could physically and mentally feel the positive changes coming, definitely mind over matter.

After dinner we had a personal hour before our scheduled night meds and vitals. I went to the onsite business center and got caught up on neglected emails as well as searched through my files and pictures stored conveniently in cyberspace. Pornography and social media network sites were blocked to say the least, but just being able to talk to my husband on a cordless phone in privacy while getting some work done made me feel like I was *still* sane, even if surrounded in a world of havoc.

That night, which was my third night, I went to bed feeling optimistic as I knew I had an early morning meeting with Dr. Lee and we would determine my discharge plan. My body was getting accustomed to the nightly low dosage medication, and for the first time in the longest time, I was developing consistency in my daily routine and I felt grounded. I had four scheduled meetings over the next 24 hours, and knowing how overwhelmingly intense they can be, I was determined to get some rest. Participation and progress were the key elements and I wanted to feel in control of my life again. It'd be foolish of me to say that I wanted things to go back to normal or to the way that they used to be, because I know that's the last thing that I wanted. It's not what I wanted to go back to, but where I want to go from there. The possibilities were infinite and I was ready for the world.

The next morning, I showered and got my day started as usual. I thought Casey was just resting while she waited for me to finish in the bathroom, but when I noticed she didn't get up for the morning medication announcement, I knew that something was out of the ordinary. Rumor had it she was being discharged later during the day, however, you still have to participate until you are officially discharged. Failure to do so can prolong your stay since several medical professional signatures are needed before you can walk out the doors to freedom.

"Case, are you okay?" I asked her as I sat at the foot of her bed.

She didn't respond and I got very nervous as by now we had all heard the tale of the girl who pressed a plastic fork into her neck and purposely ran into the wall, damaging a major artery and bleeding out. They found her body in the room the following morning and she'd been dead for hours, which is why cutlery can't be removed from the cafeteria.

I tapped Casey on the shoulder gently as her face was beneath her pillow. My touch startled her, and I apologized for the scare. She informed me that she was feeling awful and just wanted to go home and get in her bed. I was relieved and while I knew she didn't stab herself to death as there were no evident signs, I couldn't rule out infamous, old-fashioned suffocation. Casey is a sweet girl and has grown on me with her innocent spirit. I proceeded to our community group meeting as scheduled.

After the short community meeting, I learned that my appointment with Dr. Lee had been pushed off until after lunch. I was furious, but I knew that I couldn't show too much emotion as it would definitely add more time to my stay, plus I was still weary as to how the whole insurance thing would work out being I hadn't been to the doctor the entire year leading up to this stay.

Luckily for me, meditation was next on the agenda and silence was essential. I closed my eyes and followed the instructor, but found myself too anxious to concentrate on the instructor as my thoughts were overpowering. Not to mention, Gary fell asleep on the mat next to me and was snoring uncontrollably loud.

After meditation, or what always seems to serve as adult "nap time", we had an hour of what was supposed to be outdoor time, but there were light rain showers, so we had to stay indoors. The group leader led us to an area filled with every board game you can imagine, along with crosswords, word searches, adult coloring books, and a gigantic life-size metal pail filled with probably thousands of colored pencils, crayons and markers.

While the set-up was very elementary to me, seeing all the games did excite me. I haven't played some of those games since I was a kid myself, and I consider myself interactive with my children as we play all types of games together on weekends. I spent the first fifteen minutes losing in UNO, then another thirty was spent playing Scrabble.

I played Scrabble with three other women, two of whom had never played the game before. Those two were not very challenging opponents. Linda, on the other hand came from a family of Scrabble champions and gave me a run for my money. I enjoyed seeing a lighter side of her as she kept her guard up always, being her character was always at question due to her deity disbelief. The game ended early due to lack of engagement from the other ladies, but it was still fun as it stimulated my brain. I wrapped up my last fifteen minutes of time coloring pages from adult coloring books and found it to be surprisingly tranquil.

Lunch was being catered by O' Charley's restaurant and delivered to us on the unit. I declined my lunch as there was too much anticipation and anxiety was getting the best of me. There were some patients who'd been there for weeks and still had no set discharge date, while other new patients were raising hell and threatening staff to be released immediately after only a couple days. One woman, who's excessive alcoholism landed her here, was in a physically abusive marriage and found being institutionalized a pacifying alternative to her abuse. Although she was scheduled for release today, she did not want to go back home, cringing at its very thought. She wanted her husband to magically change overnight, yet sadly, he wouldn't change unless it was something that *he* desired to do as a man.

Dr. Lee and I met as scheduled after lunch. He provided me with a lot of positive feedback from the various discussion leaders regarding my progress, and assessed my current state of mind, commending me on my poise and intelligence. I told him that being at the facility put a lot of things into perspective for my life as far as direction goes. I had a clearer vision of what I wanted and what I needed, and I was prepared for a journey both challenging and fulfilling for my growth and development.

I was full of optimism and hope for the future. We agreed that today would be my last day and he would sign off on the discharge papers in the morning. I was thrilled, although I had to play it cool. He stated that he wanted to follow-up in a month as well as keep me on the medication as it would ultimately help regulate my emotions. My current dosage was only a trial to see how my body would react. Upon discharge, my dosage levels would slightly increase to provide a suffice amount.

When the meeting ended, I couldn't wait to spread the good news as I made potential lifetime connections with several of the men and women. The reaction was bittersweet for the most part, and even astonishing to some, as my length of stay was comparably short. I didn't entertain the negativity as I knew my purpose for being there was to begin the voyage of freeing myself from the pains of the past, and while I'm not instantaneously cured, I do know and believe that I'm holding this emotional weight as a personal choice.

I don't know when I'll be ready to let go completely, but I trust that whenever the time does come, I'll at least know how. I'll do so by accepting the truth for what it is, and understanding that there is beauty behind every trial and in believing that light will always come after the darkness. One of my favorite quotes is from singer John Lennon, "Living is easy with eyes closed, misunderstanding all you see."

Chapter 9

THE CHOICE

RETURNING TO REALITY was becoming my reality and the moment I waited for became the moment I began to dread. TJ was there to pick me up on time and it would be a lie if I said I didn't miss him, and it pained me to know that my feelings for Lenny were still there.

"Where is my truck?" I asked as he picked me up in his vehicle.

"It's parked on my client's lot in Millington. I'm headed to a jobsite, but we can pick it up after I'm done," he said to me.

I was infuriated, but knew that I had to work on controlling my emotions. When I finally charged my phone enough to power it on, I wished I'd prepared myself mentally for the countless voicemails and text message alerts.

I went into immediate panic mode as I couldn't mentally handle the overload. *What would I say to people? Should I lie? Should I tell the truth? Will I confirm their suspicions of insanity?* So many people were neglected over the last five days, and while I shouldn't have been disappointed, it still saddened me that I had zero missed calls from Lenny. I wanted nothing more than to smoke and have a stiff drink, but I knew that I couldn't mix my prescription meds with drugs or alcohol. The ride home confirmed that the resentment didn't cease, as I knew it would take time. TJ was super nice to me and while I reciprocated the affection, he and I both knew that it lacked authenticity.

The very next day I was scheduled to return to work and I was thrilled as I genuinely missed everyone, being we are such a close-knit group. I was scheduled to be there at two o'clock in the afternoon and my adrenaline had me up and ready by noon.

Where's my truck at? I thought as I looked outside and only saw my mom's car parked. It was only noon, so I didn't panic. I called TJ but my calls and texts went unanswered for over an hour. I tried my best to remain calm, but things just didn't make sense to me. He finally sent me a text telling me to be ready to roll in ten minutes as my truck was *still* in Millington and I would have to be dropped off at work.

Despite being furious, there was nothing that could be done about it at that point as I had to be at work in a little under an hour. Ten minutes turned into thirty minutes and I knew in my heart that if he didn't pull up that very next second, chances of me being on time my first day back were very slim. I called him again and was told that he was turning at the light by the house. I was already outside waiting as I'd been under the assumption he would've been back.

After another ten minutes or so passed it was officially two o'clock. My calls and texts were back to being ignored. My job began to call me shortly after, but I didn't answer as I couldn't bear the disappointment. I took another dose of my once-a-day medication ... then another dose. I just wanted to feel numb ... emotionless.

"You startled me. I can't believe you've been outside this long. I thought you left for work over an hour ago!" my mom exclaimed as she walked towards her car. I hurried and tried to wipe my face free of worry.

"Nope. Still waiting but it's okay, he's just up the street, no worries."

"Do you want to take me to work and you just keep my car? You can just pick me up when you get off. I don't mind waiting for you to get there," she said to me.

While the thought of it was tempting, I really didn't want to be *seen* driving so soon. I declined her offer and assured her that everything was under control, although the look in my eyes revealed the truth. She proceeded to work, and I stood at the foot of the driveway until she disappeared from my eyesight.

I opened the pill container once more and put another tablet into my mouth. My cell phone rang again. I filled my mouth with the remaining of my Red Bull. It wasn't my husband or my job ... it was my teen daughter in New York. Unfortunately, it took for her to be out of reach for me to see and understand how lost my baby really was. I wish she understood the depth of her beauty and strength. She wants so bad to fit into the world's perception of beautiful, desiring it to the point of compromising her character. She wants to be loved and understood. I understand her perfectly because she's a part of me, and more importantly, she needs me. There are very few opportunities for second chances, but if you are given one, you must seize it as if it'll never come back. As a parent, I have an obligation, a commitment to prepare my children for the world, and if I fail in doing so, then I fail the test of my chosen path.

My daughter sent me an immediate text after I rejected her call: "Hey ma! I just got this mad strange feeling and wanted to check on you. I love you and call me when you get this message."

I closed my eyes and tears streamed down my cheeks. The pill was dissolving slowly into the Red Bull that I held in my mouth. I spat the mixture onto the fall leaves that covered my yard. My cell phone rang again, and it was TJ. I didn't answer. He sent me a text stating that he was halfway home when he realized he left *my* truck keys on the cooler and had to turn around, but not to worry as he was less than two minutes away.

I wanted to believe him, but I couldn't. I called my job and told them I wasn't comfortable driving so soon and would be there shortly as I had to turn around and wait on my husband to leave work and pick me up, just so I could buy some time. I was so tired of lying. I was so tired of being a victim of circumstances. After another five minutes or so passed, I decided to just find my own way to work. I used my home Wi-Fi to set-up an Uber account as I stood in the driveway smoking my third Black & Mild. I secured my home and then proceeded to walk to the bus stop. I really didn't have a game plan, but standing still looking sad wasn't getting anything accomplished. I walked around the winding residential roads until I reached the main street.

I was too mad to determine if I was walking irregularly fast or if he was driving unusually slow, but I saw TJ zoom past me like a dashing cheetah until he realized it was me. He did a U-turn in the middle of the street and drove alongside me as I walked. I had my headphones in my ear and my music blasting as I sang aloud to my tunes, acting as if he wasn't there, although I heard every word he said. He insisted that I was over-reacting and demanded me to get inside.

I honestly felt very foolish and I knew I had to think rationally as time was of the essence. There was no way I could logically get to work any sooner, so options were limited. He sped so fast getting me there, I just knew he'd get a traffic ticket or worse, get us into a terrible accident. He thought that I'd be intimidated by his reckless driving, but I wasn't afraid. The entire ride was silent as there was nothing left to be said between he and I.

At my request, he dropped me off on the side of the building. I was already over an hour late, so a few more minutes wouldn't hurt. I wanted a few extra minutes to fix my face and get myself together. He rolled the window down and called my name to get my attention.

"You'll have your truck up here before you get off and I will be out the house this weekend because all I seem to do is disappoint you," he said to me right before driving off. *Why would he wait until I get out to say something so redundant?*

When I walked inside, I went undetected for about thirty seconds, but when my presence was made known, the atmosphere immediately changed. I felt like I was in a live taping for a scene of the "Stepford Wives." Everyone stood there waving and smiling at me warmly, welcoming me back one at a time. I went to the computer to log-in and found my hands shaking uncontrollably. My eyes were red and puffy and I pretended to yawn so I would just appear sleepy. When I opened my mouth, my jaws instantly locked in place and I began to experience muscle stiffness. *What in the world is going on with me?*

I walked to the break room to put my things into my locker. My supervisor Grace walked in behind me and asked if I were okay. Before I could force another lie out, I found myself fighting with my tears. *Please don't fall, please don't fall. You can do this!* I pleaded with myself, but it didn't work. I couldn't hold back my tears.

"Do they know?" I asked her.

"God no! Do you know how much trouble *I* would be in? Nobody knows a thing, not even Trish or Aaliyah. Everyone just misses you and was worried, especially considering both your mom and husband called saying they last saw you before heading to work and couldn't get in touch with you. I couldn't tell anyone anything more than you were alive and would be returning to work in due time. They'll only know what *you* tell them at this point."

"Everyone is acting all weird towards me, just smiling and staring, and I can just feel the millions of questions coming my way."

"Calm down. Again, they are just happy to have you back. Now take a few minutes to pull yourself together and I will bring everyone into my office, one by one, and tell them to not ask you any personal questions regarding your absence."

"Thank you. I appreciate you." She smiled at me.

"Are you sure you're okay?" she asked again as she noticed my intense shaking.

I couldn't dare tell her about my asinine scare earlier with the pills. I simply told her that it was probably a side effect of my medication and to have no worries. She urged me to take the medications with caution and to educate myself about them as much as I could, then determine on my own if I feel it's the best choice for *my* life.

I still wasn't officially on the clock, so I went out back for a quick smoke and to clear some mental space. My peaceful moment was interrupted by the startling sound of extreme bass. I opened my eyes and saw Lenny. He walked past me as if I were invisible. It was like I was nothing to him. I immediately sent him a "Hey stranger!" text and he didn't reply. A few minutes later he walked past me again, this time his face was glued to his phone and his dimples were deeper than lake Tahoe. I knew that he saw my message, he just chose to dismiss it.

As evident as the truth may have been, the hurt and rejection continued. My anger and resentment towards my husband remained consistent. Though I knew Lenny had no real desire to be with me the way he once pretended to, I would still randomly accept his late-night invites after he finally got the courage to approach me one lonely night, rocking his world then returning to mine. I thought that it would make me feel like I really won because I was still able to sleep with him, but I lost a piece of my soul with each encounter.

Sadly, I knew that his heart was elsewhere and a part of me wanted to believe that I was worth more than a consolation prize. I was at a point where I found myself willing and ready to be who and what this man wanted, and I had no logical reason as to why anymore. I was freely giving the grand prize to the runner up. Yes, he opened my heart to be receptive to purely love again, but maybe discovering that was the hidden beauty of his role in my life.

My life thus far was spent being my own worst enemy. I always knew that I had a certain degree of physical beauty, but I've always felt unworthy in a sense. I spent so much of my time and energy being a people-pleaser, catering to any and every man who showed me what I believed was genuine affection. Time after time I exhausted myself in the hopes of attaining my happily ever after or my knight in shining armor. I held onto the most abusive and scarring relationships out of fear of rejection, fear of the future, fear of being exposed as the emotionally vulnerable soul that I am. Self-love was obsolete and with every reflection lacked affection. I tried to overshadow my inability to love myself by loving anyone but myself.

While most girls grow up with big dreams, I only dreamt of being a mother. I thought that if I created life and birthed life into the world, I would have someone who always and unconditionally loves me and needs me and vice-verse. I didn't dream about getting married then starting a family. I didn't dream about going to college first so I could support this child financially. I didn't dream that my emotional instability and bitterness would be present in my parenting. I just simply wanted someone to love always, and someone to love me always.

I was always on an emotional roller coaster and I've always felt misunderstood. How could I expect someone else to do what I never dared do? It's not that I didn't want *to* love me. I just didn't know how to. Something had to give, and I had nothing left in me to give. I couldn't continue compromising morals and values to keep people in my life who did not have my best interest at heart. Why would I want someone in my life who didn't treat me with the love and respect I deserved? Why was I willing to chase a dream that only made a fool of me? Was I that scared of being alone? Or was the bigger fear accepting and finding contentment in solitude?

There is no worse feeling than feeling like you're going through something alone, or that feeling that no one else relates to or understands you. Oftentimes, I found myself obsessing over social media as it brought a temporary relief to know that there is someone else out there more "jacked-up" than me. However, it never changed anything, and it didn't add the value I desired to my life. It amazes me how we want and expect truth and honesty, yet we inadvertently lie to ourselves. We can have what may seem to be the weight of the world on our shoulders, yet we instill it in our subconscious that we're "okay, fine, and great". We repeat these lies until they become our false truths. We masquerade our pain, we bury our hurt, and we expect wounds to be healed promptly, despite the depth of the laceration.

If I said that walking away was easy, it wasn't. I'm a human being and my flesh is weakened by temptation, and it's usually those moments when I'm most vulnerable that it seems to be tested, but it's all in how I choose to respond. Was my willpower tested? Most certainly. Did I pass every test? I wish I could tell you that I did, but I didn't. I can remember telling myself that I was over Lenny, yet thoughts of him haunted my mind like a ghost. Whenever he would call I would answer desperately, journeying to him regardless to the time of day or night. Seductive pictures, money, drugs, whatever he wanted, I'd find a way to make it happen at whatever cost.

The anxiety of not knowing when he'd text or when I'd see him drove me crazy. So many times, he'd tell me we'd hook up and I'd rearrange my entire day just to be blown off without a single word or apology, only to forgive him and allow him to do the same thing over and over again, and the cycle never stopped. However, I do know that the universe has a way to reveal truth and remove obstacles from your life when you are destined for greatness, and there will be nothing that you will have to do in the process.

Lenny was unfortunately caught up in the wrong crowd and became guilty by association. As a result, he was incarcerated, but I continuously believed in his potential. Still, he continued to lie without a conscious, as if I was nothing to him. I began to see him for who he was, and I eventually had to open up my pretty brown eyes and stop depriving myself of my happiness. I chose to let go and haven't looked back since.

I knew that beating myself up would change nothing, so I didn't waste my time. While the love that I gave wasn't reciprocated, I refused to deprive my children of the love that they deserved; the mother that they deserved. Without words, they could feel my emotions, and with love I wanted to fill their hearts. I got so selfishly caught up into my own world that I neglected the biggest part of mine. I wanted to be a better mother, but I felt like I was just chasing time ... and I could never seem to catch up. I felt that no matter how much I got

Chapter 10

THE FORGIVENESS

I 'VE ALWAYS HAD this desire for more and it was only to fill what I presumed was missing. A wise man once told me that dissatisfaction is the mother of all change, and it took me being totally dissatisfied with the nothing that I was receiving, for me to begin to remove myself from those toxic situations. Believe it or not, when there is a plan, a purpose for your existence, the universe somehow manages to align the things and people in your life imperative to your growth and success, as well as remove the things and people that are not complimentary along the way.

Change means *"to give a different position, course, or direction to."* It's fair to say that it's irrational to do something the same exact way and expect a different result. When a person has a desire to become different, to become something greater, they began to see things from a different light. *Change* is a verb for a reason; because it's something that you do. For so long I wished and hoped for a change but wasn't ready to make the necessary adjustments in my life to receive that change.

I'm not here to judge as it's not my place, and more importantly, no one is perfect. Over time I've learned to accept my flaws and imperfections as they are some of my greatest motivators. I now know that it's perfectly okay to sometimes not be okay, just as it's okay to ıke a step back to mentally analyze what went wrong and determine what could've been done differently.

We all have our own reasons behind *why* we do certain things, and I can vividly recall my waking moment. *I have to break the cycle and make the best decision for my life*, I thought as I looked at my daughters asleep in their purple bunk beds. They're so precious to me and I'd rather they see me strong and possibly alone, than to see me living a life not spiritually and emotionally fulfilling. I had no money saved up and no real back up plan, but I had a vision for a future where my children see mama crying no more tears of pain, but tears of joy, freedom and happiness.

Once I learned *what* it was that I needed to do to break the cycle and find my way, I knew that it would take divine strength to overcome many of my remaining obstacles and struggles. I lost myself when I gave up on myself. When I gave up on myself, a part of me gave up on my faith, although I will never truly admit it. I was disappointed in myself for my decisions, and another part of me had some resentment towards God.

I felt that if God really cared then why would He allow longsuffering? Instead of finding beauty, I would seek pain. Instead of choosing the sensible option, I would purposely and insanely choose the more perilous one, knowing the potential risks. It was almost as if I was on a small boat alone in the big ocean, no food, no life jacket, and no ability to swim. I can either paddle towards the land within eye sight, or I can keep paddling in the direction of the unknown. The smartest thing to do would be to travel to land where possible food and safety awaits, yet with the infinite possibilities out there in the depths of the endless waters, I find myself contemplating on going astray as I fantasize about the mystery of the unseen.

When you look at the sky, the trees, the mountains, the division of the waters apart from land, the brilliance of the human body, there is so much beauty and craftsmanship that it'd be irrational to believe it just *'exists'* on its own with no celestial intelligence behind it. Faith is the substance of things hoped for and the evidence of things not seen. While there will always be questions unanswered, I refuse to believe that human life was created without a purpose. He who lacks vision, lacks purpose. My journey is a part of my divine purpose for existence and when I came to understand those elements, when I came to understand that those things happened for a reason greater than me, I was able to renew my faith. It is not that God wasn't there during my trials and storms, it was my understanding of His plan that wasn't adequate.

Before I could forgive anyone else and truly mean it, I had to forgive myself. I had to remind myself that despite the many choices I made, God was not angry with me and God truly has amazing grace. I knew the beliefs of my heart and as a result, I knew that He forgave me, and because of that, nothing else mattered. I acknowledge that my fear of life has held me back from living my life. Furthermore, I recognized that I didn't want to make another decision or take another step on my own. If God wasn't in it and beside me, it would be destined to be destroyed over time, and time was that one thing I learned to respect and appreciate.

Accepting that I was forgiven and accepting that I was willing and wanting to forgive myself were critical. It was one of the most difficult and personable challenges I faced. Every day was like a battle, but when there are forces greater than man involved, there is nothing that can stand in the way. I could feel myself changing. I could feel myself growing, and it scared me. I wanted to be different, to be better. The more I got in touch with the depths of my faith, the more my limits were tested and removed. It's so easy to fall back into old bad habits, but it only takes that small dose of reality to come back to your senses and not lose sight of the bigger picture.

The word *forgive* means, "to stop feeling anger toward someone or about something; to give up resentment." Knowing and appreciating that you've been forgiven by someone is a beautiful, cherishing experience, but knowing that you truly forgave someone is immeasurable.

Forgiveness is not about pretending that something didn't occur; forgiveness is a choice. Forgiveness is about understanding that something happened (for what may be reasons unknown) *and choosing* to not allow that circumstance to define you.

Truly forgiving someone not only benefits that person's spiritual and emotional health, but it brings about a certain unattainable, harmonic peace to you. Imagine it as being chained to a metal pole grounded in cement, and after days and days of assiduously trying to break free, you relinquish control. Simultaneously, this powerful force comes over you and it allows you to break free effortlessly. Imagine the joy, victory, and relief that it would bring! That is what truly forgiving someone feels like to me.

Forgiving others and letting them know you've forgiven them is powerful and life-changing. What good is forgiving someone for something and they never know it? To what victory do you really have when another lives with regret? What we have is right here in front of us, and it will not wait on us to decide the right thing to do. It will move beyond us while we stand in the same spot, holding onto the same pain, which may later lead to your lifelong regret. Life is short, and it takes entirely too much energy to be hateful and spiteful. Please believe me when I say that it's not a good feeling to know that you will never have another opportunity to say "I'm sorry" or "I love you" or even "Goodbye," because the one you loved has fulfilled their purpose here and moved on to the next dimension.

We all have a very limited time here on Earth and it only makes sense to use it towards peaceful, practical resolutions. The past cannot be changed, and the future is unknown, but what we can control is whether or not we choose to forgive in the presence that exists before us. Before my father turned to that dark place, he used to have a theory that '*if* we're made from god, *then* that makes us gods'.

While I do believe that there is *some* truth in its underlying meaning, I simply can agree that because of my belief that we indeed are created by God, the Spirit of God dwells within each of us. However, it does not make us the Alpha/Omega. Oftentimes we underestimate the given power of the Spirit within us, causing us to fret and fear. Having been created from God doesn't make us immortal on Earth, but it makes us capable of doing the things that we doubt the most and finding that faithful place within to bring it to its fearless fruition. As selfishly as it may seem, sometimes you must forgive other people, not for them, but for your own serenity. No person is worth such a powerful and fearful stronghold over your mind, so never fear forgiveness. Your fear is only as powerful as the strength and power you've given it. When you allow your mind and your spirit to be free from elongated affliction and oppression, you begin to take authority and gain control of your own happiness and personal destiny. Regardless to the battles lost along the way, the victory is in winning the war, and as the captain of *your* battleship, you must always choose to stay on course.

When I made the sound decision to forgive the people in my life who I allowed to affect me the most, it was one of the most terrifying yet electrifying feelings I'd ever experienced. I initially planned to write individual letters expressing my feelings, but I didn't want anything to be misinterpreted. I put my faith in God and I trusted that with each encounter *He* would allow my mouth to produce the necessary words to articulate my thoughts respectively. That is what I trusted and that is what happened in each situation.

Forgiveness is like freeing your captured soul. I started where my heart was wounded the deepest … I started with my father. I have held onto an extreme amount of bitterness, rejection, and resentment towards my father for over fifteen years and its intensity has only magnified with time. I felt that because my father didn't show us a positive example of what a man, a husband, a provider was supposed to be and do, it was a major contributing factor. It reflected in the poor choices both my older sister and I continuously made when it came to men and just life over the years. In addition, I felt that my mother was fearful of him during their marriage, so I always opted to stay in my place and comply, even when I knew I was being led astray.

Almost every man I encountered in my past had some resembling qualities of my father, and it wasn't the ones that brought tender memories and warmth to my heart, but the ones that disgusted me and pained me. My father lived with us for four months in early 2018. It was the most awkward, long four months of my life. I wanted him to change but he was still the same. I became a stranger in my own home and not only did my bills and stress level increase, but he appeared at peace being at the core of my chaos. I felt trapped and knew that it would continue to go on if I allowed it to. It was just a repeat of history and in the past, it has gotten both verbally and physically abusive with him being under the same roof.

With that being said, I decided to schedule a sit down with both of my parents, along with my sister in New York being phoned in. I chose to open up about how building a good relationship with them was critical for me, although there has always been a closeness between my mom, sister and me. I disseminated specific information of my childhood relevant to proving certain points, and made certain to not point the blame, although it was challenging at times. I can remember pouring out my heart that day to only be told by my father that I am not defined, shaped or even molded by my past and I can't continue to use that as an excuse or as a crutch for my lack of success.

I was appalled at his statement as he strongly defended it, exhibiting that he truly believed it. There were countless examples that came to my mind, but what came to my heart is what I spoke.

"While *you* determine your destiny, you're at heart a natural product of your environment. While this is by no means a form of justification, I do believe that *how* you were raised as a child and young adult subsequently plays a major part in your choices as you go through life. You can't learn to do better until you have an understanding of why you deserve to be the best *you* that you can be. If a person doesn't feel that something needs to be fixed, then they'll less likely take measurements to make a change."

I apologized to my family for being so distant over the years and asked for their forgiveness. More importantly, I acknowledged to both of my parents that I forgave them and wanted to work on building solid relationships. I forgave myself for the built-up anger and unspoken expectations. Over the course of the conversation, we had our differences along with moments of rage, but we also had moments of laughter and genuine forgiveness, and for that I'm forever merciful as that is what we have all so passionately longed for.

After committing to get my faith back on track in the right direction, and learning to forgive from the heart, I knew that the battle was only half way won. For the first time in forever, I was next on my list. Seeing people in more than one dimension has always been my gift and curse. My vision was to become the best version of me I could be, and my plan was to do so by getting to know me better.

"What do you see when you look in the mirror?" I asked myself aloud as I stood looking into a door length mirror with nothing separating me from me.

"Nappy hair, chubby cheeks, flabby stomach…"

No, I must think positive, empowering thoughts.

"Thick hair, beautiful smile, curvy," I said almost as if I was questioning myself.

I took a step closer towards the mirror, probing carefully. "Look beyond the physical, who are you at heart?"

"I'm compassionate, intuitive, and free-spirited." I smiled.

For every adjective that I called out, I wrote it down on a small sticky note and stuck it to the mirror. I initially struggled and found it difficult to get beyond three, but I didn't beat myself up as progression was the key. Instead of thinking by habit, I began to think by choice. I set a goal to add-on at least one positive adjective each day, for thirty days. Not only was this powerful for me, but I could see the positive effect that it had on my children as well. I was contagious with positivity and wanted to spread it all over the world.

My focus was not on what I needed to change about me or what I disliked about me because true change begins within the mind. My focus shifted to, "what would I do differently to produce a different result?"

I've struggled with rapid weight gain and weight loss alternatively since I had my fraternal twins ten years ago. Yes, it is easy and equally unhealthy to lose weight simply by choosing to not eat or stressing myself out to the point of being repulsed by the thought of food. However, I wanted to produce a different result, so I had to take a different course of action.

Instead of starving myself and skipping meals, I began eating smaller, more frequent portions to control my appetite. I found myself cooking more too, versus eating fast food 24/7. Over time I felt the internal difference it began to make. It was a challenge and it still is, but once I began to gain control of my appetite through discipline, I began to have more natural energy, putting me in a better overall spirit. I adjusted my water intake gradually and even added some workout routines to the mix, joining a local gym.

It was only logical to nourish my body to look and feel good from the inside out. I knew the results wouldn't be immediate, and to this day it's still a work in progress. I have my moments of struggle and crave, but I also know that it is vital that I set an example of healthy living for my children. The weight accumulated over time, so getting back to a healthy physical state is going to take hard work and time, not the surgical alteration of God's creation. I'm determined, and you cannot defeat a determined mind.

With determination being a major key contributor, changes in my life began to occur unexplainably rapid. As I said before, the changes were real. I could feel the new me resinating, just wanting to burst out, but I couldn't allow myself to be overwhelmed with anxiety, causing me to unleash abruptly or prematurely. It's as if I was given a new walk and a new talk and only like-minded souls could comprehend my language.

My habits began to change, along with my choice in music, entertainment and even friends. Just as you should be cautious of what you put into your body, you should be equally cautious as to what you feed the mind and spirit. As I discovered who I was, I turned away from the past with nothing but optimism. I seek to not be defined by where I've been, but by where I'm going and how God uses me to get there. I am at a place called beautiful, and although I still at times find myself surrounded by pandemonium, there is this undying flame that lights a peace within me.

When you become in tune with your purpose for being put here on Earth, you will understand the value of your worth. I can remember the first time I was simply referred to as *Queen*. I received it immediately because I know who I am at heart, just as I know that it takes a like-minded and equally yoked person to appreciate your inner beauty and worth. You must be in the company of those going in the same direction as you. It's far easier to hitchhike a ride with someone traveling in the same direction as you than it is to find someone willing to travel in the opposite direction.

The reality is that most people expect reciprocity, or should I say, something for something. I can recently recall my middle daughter buying Girlscout cookies from a schoolmate for four dollars a box. She gave the classmate money for three boxes of cookies, one for her and her twin siblings. Well, the little girl only delivered two boxes of cookies. My daughter took it upon herself to keep one box of cookies and gave the other box to the sibling of *her* choice. I was outraged at how she, at the age of twelve, handled the situation and I wasn't having it!

I expected her to be more logical, but maybe I was being irrational for assuming she should have mastered a lesson never taught. I explained to her that she performed a business transaction and when you do business with someone, there are principles involved.

I said to her, "Suppose you go to the store and put your favorite snacks in a basket. When you get to the checkout you pay for them with your hard-earned allowance. The cashier tells you 'thank you', keeps your groceries, and moves on to the next customer. It would make you frustrated, angry and maybe even demanding to say the least. The bottom line is, there must be decency and order in everything that you do."

Chapter 11

THE PURPOSE

A s I traveled down the road of self-discovery, I couldn't overlook that this was not all about me. Yes, this is *my* life, but I know that my purpose here is greater than me. Great is *He* who is within me, and I could feel my sense of purpose as surely as I could place my hand across my chest and feel my heart beating. The intensity of its force was overwhelming and at times the thought of not fulfilling that purpose pained me, but I refused to continue to allow fear to be a hindrance to fulfilling my destiny.

There is a blessing behind every lesson and there is power in forgiveness. The further I walked onto my destined path, the more I frequently stumbled across obstacles. Nevertheless, there were always signs of hope in those moments of doubt and despair; always that little notion to remind me to stay focused and know *I got this,* and not because of who I am, but because of Whose I am.

Just as there is power in forgiveness, there is equivalent power in prayer. I made the mistake of praying without being specific, and in life you must inspect what you expect. A lot of times we ask God for a general request and then complain when we get what *we* asked for, as we expected Him to read our minds and deliver unspoken specifics, and it's not that it wasn't possible, it just wasn't what *you* asked for.

You must say what you mean and mean what you say, and you must do so in accordance to *His* will.

There have been many times when I thought my prayers went unfulfilled, but through evolution and understanding, I learned that in most cases I just wasn't spiritually ready for what I was praying for. I have now learned to be specific in how I pray as well as in what I pray for. I've learned to pray with understanding and to pray with purpose. A woman can easily pray to God to send her a husband and He delivers her exactly what she asks for ... just *a husband*. She didn't ask God to prepare her heart and mind to be equivalently ready to receive a loving, strong providing, protective, faithful, God-fearing husband, she just simply asked for a husband with no preferences or expectations. She received the minimal and becomes angry with God when He only gave her what she asked for, as she wasn't ready for the true unspoken desires of her heart.

There is no greater hell than to live a life unfulfilled. When you intentionally live your life with purpose, you will learn exactly what it is that you need and how to achieve it. You will be slow and specific in speech, and you will not compromise as you'll know exactly what direction you're heading in. I've learned to speak from my heart when I pray, even when I don't quite know what words I should say.

Nevertheless, despite how much I struggled with reconnecting to God in the past, I know that I must continue to take the steps to maintain the alignment of my personal choices in accordance to His will for my life. I can't put flour alone in the oven and expect a pastry masterpiece, just as I can't expect a change and be willing to stay the same. It's like praying for prosperity yet you never express compassion or generosity. If God can't trust you with what little you *think* you have, why on Earth would He trust you with an increase? Would your supervisor give you a promotion for being a mediocre employee? No, you would earn your promotion because they recognize your growth and strength as the most qualified candidate.

Understanding the power and importance of forgiveness can take your spirituality to new heights. When you seek for a deeper understanding, you become not only more in touch with your faith, but yourself as well. The power of discernment was placed upon my spirit when I learned the significance behind forgiveness. In that, I began to discover a more in depth purpose for my existence. I've always been very intuitive, but it was as if my gift was enhanced with precision and clarity ... I felt like a superhero or an angelic being.

At first, I assumed that forgiveness meant you *must* accept what another person does or says regardless to the extent of the hurt, but it doesn't mean that. I believe that it means you consciously acknowledge that something was done or said, it cannot be undone, and you choose to not hold that mistake over that person's head. However, it doesn't force you to keep that person in your life as only you know your level of tolerance and more importantly, your worth. The choices we make, big and small, help determine the direction of our destiny. The gift of life is so precious, and it should be handled with sagacity and delicacy. Some people are meant to be in our lives for a short moment, while others for a lifetime. Alongside being unjust, it is unfair to choose to live in misery or to force someone else to live in misery when their season in your life has passed.

In the past, I oftentimes found myself holding onto hope for years to come, and it mentally exhausted me. We are only who we are as an individual and you can't be everybody's *everything*. Letting go hurts like hell, but its healing is therapeutic for the soul. Letting go strengthens the heart and not in a cold way, but in a manner that represents growth, maturity and inner strength. Time and prayer heals wounds and if I've learned nothing else, I've learned the importance of patience. The universe does not revolve around me and I can't expect deep wounds to heal overnight like they do on the screens of Hollywood. Learning to love and trust takes time and so does learning to emotionally heal and let go.

Traveling down the road of self-discovery can definitely get lonely at times as you sometimes seem to lose more than you gain on the surface, but it's one of the most amazing journeys. Additionally, as you journey closer to where you're destined to go, it'll be revealed that nothing you lost along the way was ever yours indefinitely as what is divinely for you can't be taken from you.

The trip to discovering you is an investment worth making and it can't be bought with a monetary price. While the beauty of the destination is priceless, the evolution lies within the journey. How do you know when you are on the right path? That is a question you will not have to ask as your peace will be incomparable and more importantly, unattainable within *your* own strength. When you discover who you are, you will gain the insight and revelation of your purpose for existence and that purpose will always be greater than you.

There will be pain in the growth and developmental process as you can't have success without sacrifice. But beautifully, it's all a part of God's divine plan as when you understand your purpose, you understand your pain had to be endured to make you stronger for what lies ahead of you. When you've been placed here to fulfill something greater than you, no matter how much you rebel or resist, you'll always find yourself being unconsciously drawn back to the very calling you are running from.

The more in touch I became with the essence of my journey, the more I understood that each and every joyful and painful moment in my life occurred for a specific reason, for a specific purpose. I came out of every occurrence with a different and unique emotion, feeling and overall perspective. With each occurrence, the clarity of its silent significance was becoming more transparent, despite my vision being circumstantially and temporarily blocked.

When you're truly able to open your eyes and see people and things for what they really are, and not just your inspiration for them, you'll have a veracious understanding of what you're engaging in. Also, you'll know how to best approach it from a realistic standpoint versus taking an idealistic approach. When you begin to learn who you are, you seek to have knowledge and understanding in who and what you're dealing with, as you'll have a stern refusal to have anything that's not complimentary to your life.

I will never forget being *disciplined* at work for being late the first time in eight months, previously recovering from a six-month attendance probationary period. I walked into the office to find my supervisor, along with a colleague to serve as a witness, presenting me with a final warning write-up. Alongside the fact that it should have only been a Level II warning, due to the length of time in between them. My supervisor modified the document right in front of me, which was originally completed by HR, to reflect *final*.

As she read it aloud, I followed along as it listed each of the three dates that I was ever late over the course of the last two years. I can remember feeling like it was judgment day and all my sins were being shown before me. It was in that very moment that I realized that no matter how great I am at *this* job, I would always be back at that questionable point, and sometimes you just have to accept things for what they are. My schedule was being constantly manipulated from one week to the next. There were minimal opportunities for advancement and my motivation for being there was becoming obsolete. I couldn't apologize for being subjective to error as I was only human, and some circumstances are beyond our control. I felt like a puppet on a string and I refused to be stringed along by anyone, anymore.

Faith and fear cannot perpetually coexist, so I did the inevitable and joyously stepped out on faith. I considered both the pro's and con's, and while I was in no financial position to afford to be jobless for any amount of time, I knew that I couldn't fulfill my purpose fearfully. I began to search various career websites for jobs. The search process was overwhelming and mentally draining.

Being a woman, let alone an African-American woman with only a two-year college degree, was like having three strikes already against me. I hated to fill out the EEO questions at the end of applications as deep down I felt that gender and race always mattered. By answering *optionally* I felt as if I was automatically disqualifying myself, and by not answering at all it would be as if I had something to conceal. Not to mention, I didn't know whether or not to include my most recent job on my resume or just have an unexplainable two-year gap, although I anticipated parting ways amicably to sustain an 'eligible for rehire' status. My voicemail flooded with soliciting calls and my inbox outpoured with fraudfully deceptive emails. I even went on a couple of dead-end marketing interviews. I was beginning to feel discouraged, but deep inside I knew that somehow, someway, it would all fall into place. I just didn't know how.

I was in desperate need of forgiveness and ultimately wanted my employer to move beyond what was unchangeable and focus on the greatness ahead, the greatness in me, but I was judged, scrutinized, and mocked for my mistakes. It hurts to *know* who you are, yet only be seen for who you were. It hurts to know that God has forgiven you, but the world can't see beyond what lies at the surface. It hurts to know that the very feeling you are experiencing, is the way you once intentionally made someone else feel.

I put in a two-week notice without securing employment from another company, and as crazy as it may seem, I felt wickedly free from bondage. No job. No money. No savings. And no fears. My inner peace was as calm as the sea on a windless day. It wasn't about giving up, but knowing when it's time to move on. A company must always act in the best interest of the business and as an individual, you equally have a responsibility to make the most ethical and morally guided choices for your life.

Faith without works is dead. Later that exact same day, I received a call with an offer from my previous employer of ten years, nearly doubling my current salary. I hadn't even put in an application for the job, but when discipline, prayer and supplication are present, possibilities become endless and faith becomes limitless. While it wasn't my dream job, it was a way to get my head above water at a rapid pace.

I fell to my knees in prayer and worship, and I can speak on these things because they are tried and true to my life. I'm stronger than I thought, and sometimes it takes having the shoe on the other foot to fully understand the nature of the situation.

While I don't believe being late and *disciplined* was necessarily my karma for being so resilient when it came down to forgiving TJ and being insensitive to his needs, it was definitely an eye opener. In life you must be fair and sometimes being fair means admitting that you were wrong and taking corrective actions to fix your mistakes. I thanked God for my financial blessing, and even though it may look as if that I was right back where I started, I felt that I was placed back there for a reason.

I first and foremost had to prove to myself that I could do it and succeed again. Moreover, it was just time for me to close that door indefinitely, but still with diligence and grace to maintain honor. I inevitably used the job as a crutch I could lean on if "need be" as I know I excelled at my leadership role and good talent was hard to find, or should I say keep.

Realistically, I also knew that I didn't want to do physical labor in an unsafe environment just to proclaim '*I make good money*' for the next thirty plus years until retiring, so it wasn't a career move. I admit that I was tired of constantly having to prove myself repeatedly, but I now understand that throughout life you will always have to prove yourself. If you want to remain in the top tier of your league, reassurance is always the fueling factor. You go to war for the people who believe in you, and you win to prove yourself to those who didn't.

Prior to me accepting the offer from my previous employer, I applied for a respected position at a prestigious financial institution. It was my ideal dream job with on-the-job training and certification, corporate benefits and a competitive salary. A month had gone by and I still hadn't heard anything definite after the first interview, except for playing email tag with the warm-spirited HR personnel. I started employment at my old job and dreaded its every minute. Not only was upper management unprofessional and demeaning, the job almost demanded me to step outside of my character to maintain respect.

I met many talented, hard-working people along the way, but I felt so out of place. Everyone was so serene being surrounded by drama and disarray. However, I could not conform to the dissatisfaction and discomfort. Stress and confusion were at an all-time high, but I gave one-hundred percent each day as I knew there was a purpose for the challenges and hardships that I was enduring, and it would be revealed in due time.

My days were long, ten to twelve-hour shifts, six days a week (salaried). I missed my daughter's first band concert recital due to scheduling, and I felt myself mentally going back to that *"place"*. I knew that I was again putting my family in a situation where there was no work-life balance. I was on the verge of giving up. Opposite from that demonic force that once told me I couldn't go on, an angelic force within lifted my spirit and told me that I couldn't give up.

The prestigious financial institution called to schedule a second interview for the position I applied for. I knew that I had to give it all that I had, and I did. I made the choice to put fear and worry aside and I was given the right words at the right time as they flowed out with ease. Although that brought a slight bit of relief, the battle was only half way won. Between the negative impact of my damaged credit and lack of credentials, the odds were against me, but I tried not to focus on the mistakes and imperfections that could possibly stand in the way of my idyllic job.

Nevertheless, I'm a firm believer that when prayers go up, blessings and miracles rain down. When something is in align with your destiny and has the potential to magnify your purpose on a scale greater than you, regardless to what the odds are, if it's for you, then it is already yours, so approach it with confidence, not caution. My faith was the guiding light and the calming voice that never failed me.

While I don't know what the future holds, I'm happy to say that I'm truly excited and I look forward to whatever it may be, as ultimately,

I hold the key. The key to happiness for me lies within the power of choice. I want the best for my life, and the situation will not change until I choose to make a difference. When I realized that my obstacles were just hidden opportunities for growth, I saw the emerge of optimism. Every choice will involve some level of compromise, and while every choice may not turn out to be a good choice, every choice will have the potential to be turned into something meaningful. We make so many choices daily that we don't realize the power we seek is already within us.

My personal goal now is to maintain a healthy and positive state-of-mind. Even if it means making those tough choices and not knowing the outcome. I want to be forgiven and seen for who I am at heart, and in doing so, I choose to be the change that I want to see. I choose to embrace the next chapter of my life. And more importantly, I choose forgiveness, as I have been forgiven.

My heart is at peace as I've been blessed with the opportunity to experience some of the most beautiful, refreshing and exhilarating sensations I've ever felt and may ever feel, but the positive energy I consumed from them is everlasting. Although I'm subjecting myself to scrutiny and vulnerability, to say I have regrets is to say that I don't embrace my struggle. Even if my *soul* purpose of enduring and overcoming is just to be able to tell my story, I couldn't be more honored to be used. Within every failure lies a hidden victory, and more importantly, there is mercy and grace in forgiveness. Learn it, Live it, Love it! #Forgive2Live

About the Author

FOR NAJAH WILLIAMS, experience is the best teacher. *Forgiven* started out as just another collection of her writing miscellany: thoughts, poems, and letters to God. Over time it came together to help her understand her truth. It made her wonder: How many other women were going through life, facing their own trial while feeling scared and alone? Thus, her decision to use her love of writing not only as a tool for self-exploration but as a way to reach out to others came to be. She lives in Memphis, Tennessee, with her four beautiful children and their Shih Tzu. She is currently formulating her second book. On life and writing, she has this to say: "We can't rewrite our past, but we do have the ability to create our own happiness by making wise, thoughtful choices." You can find Najah online at najahwilliams.com.

CPSIA information can be obtained
at www.ICGtesting.com
Printed in the USA
LVHW091903140419
614156LV00001B/1/P